Contents

General introduction   xi

Poetry detectives   xiii

1 Opening eyes   **1**

On My Short-Sightedness   3
Prem Chaya

The Blind Man at the Fair   4
Joseph Campbell

The Blind Boy   5
Colley Cibber

First Sight   6
Philip Larkin

Hares at Play   7
John Clare

Kob Antelope   8
Anonymous (translated by Ulli Beier)

Mountain Lion   9
D. H. Lawrence

Red Kites Rising   12
Philip Gross

The Fly   13
William Blake

Acts of God   14
Catherine Phil MacCarthy

Mawu of the Waters   15
Abena P. A. Busia

The Ferryboat and the Traveller   16
Han Yong-Un

The Fridge   17
Boris Slutsky (translated by Elaine Feinstein)

The Inside of Things   18
Brian Patten

The Seed Shop   19
Muriel Stuart

Gunpowder Plot   20
Vernon Scannell

'They'   22
Siegfried Sassoon

Activities   23

2 You and me   **31**

One   33
James Berry

Friendship   34
Cole Porter

Friendship   36
Elizabeth Jennings

Heroes   37
Benjamin Zephaniah

These I Have Loved   38
Rupert Brooke

Unburglars   39
Philip Gross

Boy at the Window   40
Richard Wilbur

Footings   41
Colette Bryce

Purge   42
Sheila Glen Bishop

Sewing Fingertips   44
Jean Sprackland

Shocks   45
Jean Sprackland

Tell Your Mother I Saved Your Life   46
Jean Sprackland

Smothering Sunday   47
John Hegley

Bringing Up a Single Parent   48
Brian Patten

In the Playground   49
Michael Rosen

Conkers   50
Grace Nichols

The Shout   52
Simon Armitage

The Apple-Raid   53
Vernon Scannell

Geography Lesson   55
Brian Patten

Mid-Term Break   56
Seamus Heaney

Night Mail   57
W. H. Auden

Activities   59

3 Out of doors   **67**

The Door   69
Miroslav Holub

Our Pond   70
Daniel Pettiward

My Neighbours' Rabbit   71
Brian Patten

My Mother Saw a Dancing Bear   72
Charles Causley

Hedgehog   73
Anthony Thwaite

Python   74
Traditional (*Nigeria*)

The Tomcat   75
Don Marquis

The Fox   77
Phoebe Hesketh

An Old Woman of the Roads   78
Pádraic Colum

Meg Merrilies   79
John Keats

The Song of Wandering Aengus   81
W. B. Yeats

Caravan   82
Jean Sprackland

The Bicycle   84
Derek Mahon

Wind Gauge   86
Gillian Clarke

Slowly, the Fog   87
F. R. McCreary

Mist   88
Douglas Gibson

Trees in the Storm   89
Brian Patten

Feeding Out-Wintering Cattle at Twilight   90
Ted Hughes

Activities   92

4 Ebb and flow   **99**

The Sea   101
James Reeves

Sea Fever   102
John Masefield

Thoughts Like an Ocean   103
Gareth Owen

Evidence   105
Eiléan Ní Chuilleanáin

Tree Stump   106
Moya Cannon

The Cherry Trees   107
Laurence Binyon

Loveliest of Trees, the Cherry Now   108
A. E. Housman

Stopping by Woods on a Snowy Evening   109
Robert Frost

The Way Through the Woods   110
Rudyard Kipling

In Time of 'The Breaking of Nations'   111
Thomas Hardy

Uffington   112
John Betjeman

Dumbshow   113
John Montague

Lucy Gray (or, Solitude)   114
William Wordsworth

In the Attic   117
Andrew Motion

Drummer Hodge   118
Thomas Hardy

High Flight (An Airman's Ecstasy)   119
John Gillespie Magee

2000 AD   120
Rabindranath Tagore

Activities   121

5 Digging deeper   **129**

There Are Days   131
John Montague

Five O'Clock Shadow   132
John Betjeman

Guardians   133
John Montague

A Dream   134
Dermot Healy

House on a Cliff   136
Louis MacNeice

In a Non-Sleeper   137
Boris Slutsky (translated by Elaine Feinstein)

Missing the Troop Train   138
Yevgeny Vinokurov (translated by Daniel Weissbort)

O What Is That Sound   140
W. H. Auden

Stanley Meets Mutesa   142
David Rubadiri

Ozymandias   145
Percy Bysshe Shelley

Call to a Simple Feast   146
Sue Minish

Charms   147
Catherine Phil MacCarthy

The Hollow Wood   148
Edward Thomas

Watching for Dolphins   149
David Constantine

The Donkey   151
G. K. Chesterton

The Tyger   152
William Blake

Activities   153

Notes on authors   **161**

Acknowledgements   170

General introduction

Poetry can be about all kinds of things, and this collection ranges over a jostling world of different subjects: the effects of being short-sighted, how irritating boys can be, friends, falling in a pond or off a wall, the power of the weather, the vastness of the sea, the sneer of a power-mad four-thousand-year-old pharaoh – they're all here! What the poems in this hugely varied collection have in common is that they open your eyes to new views of the world. They do this through the poets' fresh perceptions of their experiences and their descriptions of how these experiences make them feel, conveyed through imaginative uses of well-chosen words.

The first section, *Opening eyes*, begins with poems that are literally about eyesight. Then there are poems about taking time to look at things properly: a hare, an antelope, a red kite rising on the wind. Later poems explore a different kind of vision, asking you to consider what it would be like to be a fly, or a river, or a ferry boat. Others explore the secret life of things – the personality of a fridge, or the chicken farm inside an egg.

You and me is about being uniquely ourselves, with our habits, and our likes and dislikes, and about all the ways in which we relate to other people: friends, heroes, family, and even burglars and snowmen. Some of the poems here are about hopes and dreams, others about loss and disappointment.

Out of doors begins with an invitation to venture out into the big, wide world, and to open ourselves to opportunity. Other poems are more obviously about the real outdoor world – about wild or unusual weather. A group of animal poems introduce us to a dancing bear, a python and a terrifying tomcat. This section also includes a number of poems about people who choose to be wanderers.

The fourth section, *Ebb and flow*, focuses on the rhythms of change, on the ebb and flow of the sea, on the seasons, on how the world changes over time, and how we change with it. A group of poems here looks at the end of life, at war, and finally at the distant future.

The final section, *Digging deeper*, features poems chosen to make you think more deeply. There are some poems notable for their atmosphere – like *Missing the Troop Train*, spoken by a lone man on a frozen railway station platform in the middle of nowhere, at night. Many of the poems here also use words in especially interesting ways. Many raise questions about life or the world we live in.

Within each section, poems on similar themes have been grouped together. All the poems stand alone, but reading several poems on one theme can add to your understanding of each individual poem.

To support your reading, certain words are explained in the footnotes. Each section concludes with a range of activities to help you explore the poets' ideas and use of language. Rather than just 'testing' you on your understanding of the poems, these are intended to encourage you to think about the ideas in the poems and how they are expressed. These activities should help you to think about the word choices made by the poets, and to enjoy writing your own poems inspired by this collection. At the very end of each section, a series of *Compare and contrast* activities provide opportunities to compare two or more texts. Notes about the authors can be found at the end of the anthology.

Poetry detectives

During the Cold War in the second half of the 20th century, Europe was divided in two by a boundary known as the Iron Curtain (the Berlin Wall was part of it). The countries on each side viewed those on the other with suspicion, and sent spies to try to find out their secrets. These spies communicated using codes and sent messages in many ingenious ways – including poetry. Some spies studied poetry so that they would be able to recognise secret information that had been hidden in poems that they had intercepted.

Most poetry does not contain secrets of national importance, but all readers are, to a certain extent, poetry detectives. Poetry is a way of expressing thoughts and feelings, and because these aren't always simple, a poem can have more than one meaning. Often, a poet chooses to express quite complex ideas by telling a story or describing a situation or object. For example, in *The Apple-Raid* (page 53), Vernon Scannell tells how he and his friends once went out stealing apples; in doing so, he also tells the reader a lot about childhood and war.

The trick to discovering the meanings of a poem is to look for little details. It is often a good idea to read the poem several times. Even if it seems very simple, hardly worth reading more than once, you will probably find things you missed on your first reading. If the poem doesn't make sense to you at first, don't worry, but think about the words the poet has used. Look beyond your first thoughts to see what other ideas are hidden in the poem.

The following tips will help you become a successful poetry detective.

Voice

A poem may be 'spoken' by one character or by several. One of these characters may be the poet him/herself, but often it is not – the poet is speaking through someone else. For example, Brian Patten wrote *Bringing Up a Single Parent* (page 48) as an adult, but the character narrating the poem is a child.

To help you think about voice when you read a poem, ask your-self these questions:

- Is the poet talking as him/herself or as another character?
- If the poet is talking as another character, why do you think he/she has chosen to do this? How does the character help the poet say what he/she wants to say?
- Do you agree with the poet's point of view?

If a poem has several characters, you might find it helpful to share the characters out and read it aloud. This can really bring a poem to life.

Mood

Mood, or atmosphere, describes how a poem makes the reader feel. When you read a poem, think about whether it makes you feel happy, or sad. Is it funny or scary? Realistic or dreamlike? Is the mood the same all the way through or does it change?

Try to work out why the poem makes you feel the way it does. Is it the subject matter, the poem's structure (e.g. whether it rhymes) or the words the poet has chosen? It could be all of these things, but sometimes they don't match up – a poem with a jaunty rhythm can sometimes be very sad. If this happens, ask yourself why the poet has chosen to do this.

Language

Sometimes the words of a poem are the type of words that you might use every day. Other words may be less familiar. It might help you to list any new or unusual words that you find and ask yourself why those particular words have been chosen. If there are any you don't under-stand, look them up in a dictionary. Do they add to the mood of the poem?

Imagery

Imagery or word pictures are ways of illustrating ideas and creating atmosphere. Images can be used in any kind of writing but are proba-bly used more frequently in poetry than prose. The most common are similes, which compare one thing to something else using the word 'like' or the word 'as', and metaphors, which describe one thing as if it were something else. An image encourages the reader to think about something in a different way – sometimes, this can be quite surprising. What do you think of the following examples?

- In *The Sea* (page 101), the sea is compared to 'a hungry dog', who 'rolls on the beach all day' and at night 'howls and hollos long and loud'. This extended metaphor runs right through the poem.
- In *The Fridge* (page 17), a fridge is spoken to as if it were a living creature with moods. It is described as 'a fine, white, self-satisfied creature' and as 'the house-dog of machinery'.

Rhyme

A poem does not have to rhyme. Often it is the poet's choice of words, and their order, that lifts a poem above everyday prose. However, many poems have an obvious rhyme scheme. Up until the middle of the 20th century, in particular, poets tended to use recognised patterns. For example, *Hares at Play* (page 7) is written in rhyming couplets (where pairs of lines rhyme):

> *The birds are gone to bed, the cows are still (a)*
> *And sheep lie panting on each old mole hill (a)*
> *And underneath the willow's grey-green bough (b)*
> *Like toil a-resting – lies the fallow plough. (b)*

If a rhyme scheme is too obvious, it can be distracting, so most poets try to make sure that the rhyming words don't leap out at the reader. Sometimes, however, a very obvious rhyme scheme can be used to humorous effect. In Cole Porter's *Friendship* (page 34), for example, you can almost guess what word is coming:

> *If you're ever in a **jam**,*
> *Here I **am**.*
> *If you're ever in a **mess**,*
> *S.O.**S**.*
> *If you ever feel so happy you end in **jail**,*
> *I'm your **bail**.*

Do you find this use of rhyme funny? Why/why not?

Other poems do use rhyme, but do not follow a formal pattern. *The Inside of Things* (page 18), for example, has only one pair of end rhymes in each verse. Notice that 'free' and 'sea' are perfect rhymes but 'farm' and 'palm' are not – they are called near rhymes.

> *Inside the dandelion seed is a clock.*
> *Inside the egg is a chicken farm; (a)*
> *Inside a fist an army awaits,*
> *Inside a kiss is an open palm. (a)*
>
> *Inside a snowflake an avalanche*
> *Trembles and waits to get free; (b)*
> *Inside a raindrop a river plots*
> *The best way to run to the sea. (b)*

Rhythm

When we speak or read, we say some words, or parts of words, more forcefully than others, creating a pattern of stressed and unstressed syllables. This is something that the poet can control through his/her choice and placement of words. Look at Benjamin Zephaniah's poem *Heroes*. Do you think it has a strong rhythm? Does it have a musical quality to it? How has the poet achieved this?

Voice, mood, language, imagery, rhyme and rhythm are all important aspects of poetry. Asking yourself questions about how the poem is put together will help you to discover its meanings. But the best way to become a successful poetry detective is simply to read as much poetry as you can!

1 Opening eyes

The poems in this section present in concentrated form what the whole collection is about – they are the result of looking at the world through fresh eyes. Some of the poems really are about eyesight; others take a close-up view of the world, revealing the kind of detail that might escape the casual observer, as in John Clare's *Hares at Play*. The poets use words to make us see what they see, evoking the vulnerability of the *Kob Antelope*, for example, and the power of the soaring birds of prey in *Red Kites Rising*.

The later poems enter the world of the 'inner eye', asking us to join the poet in seeing both living and inanimate things from a different angle. Some even challenge us to imagine ourselves as these things, as in Han Yong-Un's poem spoken in the patient voice of a ferry boat.

Activities

1 Several of the poems in this section are about seeing things in a fresh or different way. A famous example of this is a poem by Craig Raine called *A Martian Sends a Postcard Home*. Here are the first few lines:

> *Caxtons are mechanical birds with many wings*
> *and some are treasured for their markings –*
>
> *they cause the eyes to melt*
> *or the body to shriek without pain.*
>
> *I have never seen one fly, but*
> *sometimes they perch on the hand.*

Can you work out the riddle in these lines: what are 'Caxtons'? What is Craig Raine talking about in lines 3 and 4?

2   Poems about animals can often 'capture' something about a creature's appearance, movement or nature through very close observation. Here are some descriptive phrases from poems in this section:

- *The head / beautiful like carved wood* (kob antelope)
- *her bright striped frost-face* (mountain lion)
- *half air / themselves in their feathers and bones* (red kites)

Discuss these phrases with a partner. Do any of them seem to 'capture' the animal for you? As a pair, try to write some short phrases to describe an aspect of an animal that you have observed. It could be a pet or an animal in the wild.

On My Short-Sightedness
by Prem Chaya

To my short-sighted eyes
The world seems better far
Than artificial aid
To sight would warrant[1] it:
The earth is just as green,
The sky a paler blue;
Many a blurred outline
Of overlapping hue;
Shapes, forms are indistinct;
Distance a mystery;
Often a common scene
Conceals a new beauty;
Ugliness is hidden
In a curtain of mist;
And hard, cruel faces
Lose their malignity.[2]
So do not pity me
For my short-sighted eyes;
They see an unknown world
Of wonder and surprise.

---

[1]**warrant** justify
[2]**malignity** evil cruelty

The Blind Man at the Fair

by Joseph Campbell

O to be blind!
To know the darkness that I know.
The stir I hear is empty wind,
The people idly come and go.

The sun is black, tho' warm and kind,
The horsemen ride, the streamers blow
Vainly in the fluky[1] wind,
For all is darkness where I go.

The cattle bellow to their kind,
The mummers[2] dance, the jugglers throw,
The thimble-rigger[3] speaks his mind –
But all is darkness where I go.

I feel the touch of womankind,
Their dresses flow as white as snow;
But beauty is a withered rind,
For all is darkness where I go.

Last night the moon of Lammas[4] shined,
Rising high and setting low;
But light is nothing to the blind –
All, all is darkness where they go.

White roads I walk with vacant mind,
White cloud-shapes round me drifting slow,
White lilies waving in the wind –
And darkness everywhere I go.

---

[1] **fluky** coming and going randomly
[2] **mummers** actors
[3] **thimble-rigger** fraudster
[4] **Lammas** Celtic summer festival

The Blind Boy

by Colley Cibber

O say, what is that thing called light,
   Which I can ne'er enjoy?
What is the blessing of the sight?
   O tell your poor blind boy!

You talk of wond'rous things you see,
   You say the sun shines bright!
I feel him warm, but how can he
   Then make it day or night?

My day or night myself I make,
   Whene'er I wake or play;
And could I ever keep awake,
   It would be always day.

With heavy sighs I often hear
   You mourn my hopeless woe;
But sure with patience I may bear
   A loss I ne'er can know.

Then let not what I cannot have
   My cheer of mind destroy.
Thus while I sing, I am a king,
   Although a poor blind boy!

First Sight
by Philip Larkin

Lambs that learn to walk in snow
When their bleating clouds the air
Meet a vast unwelcome, know
Nothing but a sunless glare.
Newly stumbling to and fro
All they find, outside the fold,
Is a wretched width of cold.

As they wait beside the ewe,
Her fleeces wetly caked, there lies
Hidden round them, waiting too,
Earth's immeasurable surprise.
They could not grasp it if they knew
What so soon will wake and grow
Utterly unlike the snow.

Hares at Play

by John Clare

The birds are gone to bed, the cows are still
And sheep lie panting on each old mole hill
And underneath the willow's grey-green bough
Like toil a-resting – lies the fallow[1] plough.
The timid hares throw daylight's fears away
On the lane's road to dust, and dance and play,
Then dabble in the grain by nought deterred[2]
To lick the dewfall from the barley's beard.
Then out they sturt[3] again and round the hill
Like happy thoughts – dance – squat – and loiter still.
Till milking maidens in the early morn
Jingle their yokes and sturt them in the corn.
Through well known beaten paths each nimbling hare
Sturts quick as fear – and seeks its hidden lair.

---

[1] **fallow** resting
[2] **by nought deterred** not put off by anything
[3] **sturt** start suddenly, startle

Kob Antelope

Anonymous (translated by Ulli Beier)

A creature to pet and spoil
like a child.
Smooth skinned
stepping cautiously
in the lemon grass.
Round and plump
like a newly married wife.
The neck
heavy with brass rings.
The eyes
gentle like a bird's.
The head
beautiful like carved wood.
When you suddenly escape
you spread fine dust
like a butterfly
shaking its wings.
Your neck seems long,
so very long
to the greedy hunter.

Mountain Lion

by D. H. Lawrence

Climbing through the January snow, into the Lobo canyon
Dark grow the spruce-trees, blue is the balsam,[1] water sounds
    still unfrozen, and the trail is still evident.

Men!
Two men!
Men! The only animal in the world to fear!

They hesitate.
We hesitate.
They have a gun.
We have no gun.

Then we all advance, to meet.

Two Mexicans, strangers, emerging out of the dark and snow
    and inwardness of the Lobo valley.
What are you doing here on this vanishing trail?

What is he carrying?
Something yellow.
A deer?

Qué tiene, amigo?[2]
León –

He smiles, foolishly, as if he were caught doing wrong.
And we smile, foolishly, as if we didn't know.
He is quite gentle and dark-faced.

---

[1]**balsam**   kind of fir tree
[2]**Qué tiene, amigo?**   What have you got, friend?

It is a mountain lion,
A long, long slim cat, yellow like a lioness.
Dead.
He trapped her this morning, he says, smiling foolishly.

Lift up her face,
Her round, bright face, bright as frost.
Her round, fine-fashioned head, with two dead ears;
And stripes in the brilliant frost of her face, sharp, fine dark
        rays,
Dark, keen, fine eyes in the brilliant frost of her face.
Beautiful dead eyes.

Hermoso es![3]

---

[3]**Hermoso es!**   It is beautiful!

They go out towards the open;
We go on into the gloom of Lobo.
And above the trees I found her lair,
A hole in the blood-orange brilliant rocks that stick up, a little
    cave.
And bones, and twigs, and a perilous ascent.

So, she will never leap up that way again, with the yellow flash
    of a mountain lion's long shoot!
And her bright striped frost-face will never watch any more,
    out of the shadow of the cave in the blood-orange rock,
Above the trees of the Lobo dark valley-mouth!

Instead, I look out.
And out to the dim of the desert, like a dream, never real;

To the snow of the Sangre de Cristo mountains, the ice of the
    mountains of Picoris,
And near across at the opposite steep of snow, green trees
    motionless standing in snow, like a Christmas toy.

And I think in this empty world there was room for me and a
    mountain lion.
And I think in the world beyond, how easily we might spare a
    million or two of humans
And never miss them.
Yet what a gap in the world, the missing white frost-face of
    that slim yellow mountain lion!

Red Kites Rising

by Philip Gross

Ease
has nothing to do with it. The wind machine
is cranking. It's a Puffing Billy[1] of a day.

High-sided vehicles quail,[2] think better
and shift down a gear as if for a gradient[3]
no one can see, and I've pulled over

at a sudden plastering of hail,
the windscreen blenching,[4] wipers
at a loss – as suddenly

cleared . . . and up a shaft
of swept sky, on a thermal[5] clean
as a piston, two rise, almost casual,

leaning to the camber[6] of the air (half air
themselves in their feathers and bones),
their wingtips nearly touching, hand-

over-hand-hauled up by double helix[7]
torque,[8] a force that looks for all the world
like ease.

---

[1]**Puffing Billy**   an early steam train
[2]**quail**   draw back in fear or pain, falter
[3]**gradient**   slope (uphill)
[4]**blenching**   drawing away, flinching
[5]**thermal**   draught of warm air
[6]**camber**   slight upward curve
[7]**double helix**   coiled structure of DNA
[8]**torque**   twisting force

The Fly
by William Blake

Little Fly,
Thy summer's play
My thoughtless hand
Has brushed away.

Am not I
A fly like thee?
Or art not thou
A man like me?

For I dance,
And drink, and sing,
Till some blind hand
Shall brush my wing.

If thought is life
And strength and breath,
And the want
Of thought is death;

Then am I
A happy fly,
If I live
Or if I die.

Acts of God

by Catherine Phil MacCarthy

When thunder crashed on the roof
like heavy furniture

I felt the way blind
downstairs in the dark,

found everyone
round the kitchen table

counting seconds.
Lightning lit the tap,

cracked the floor like a whip,
made me jump out of my skin.

The unconcerned outline
of my father's shoulders,

my mother somewhere
foraging[1] for matches,

the pitch of my sisters'
voices, the baby upstairs

sleeping – small things
that hold us.

Then in the hush
a downpour.

---

[1]**foraging**   searching

Mawu of the Waters
by Abena P. A. Busia

With mountains as my footstool
   and stars in my curls
I reach down to reap[1] the waters with my fingers
and look! I cup lakes in my palms.
I fling oceans around me like a shawl
and am transformed
into a waterfall.
Springs flow through me
and spill rivers at my feet
as fresh streams surge to make seas.

---

[1]**reap**   cut or gather, harvest

The Ferryboat and the Traveller

by Han Yong-Un

I am a ferry boat. A traveller, you tread on me
with muddy shoes. I take you aboard to cross
the river. With you held in my arms, I go across
the currents, deep, shallow or rapid.
If you do not turn up, I await you from dawn
to dusk, despite the wind, rain or snow.
Yet, once you've crossed the river, you do not
look back on me. But I believe you will be coming
back some day.
I grow old and worn-out waiting for you
day after day.
I am a ferryboat. You are a traveller.

The Fridge

by Boris Slutsky (translated by Elaine Feinstein)

What a sturdy square block of a thing you are!
Such a fine, white, self-satisfied creature!

Sometime you stand dumb as a boulder
or drop off into a cold sleep, or
sometimes your metal belly rumbles, but there's
no point in working out your meaning.

Of all machines the fridge must be the
most good-natured; hog-fat and
roomy as a snow-drift, it
must be said to hold the purest heart.

Firmly under human domination[1]
even the cold that creeps out from it
is only a small cold blast, too small
to threaten any freeze-up of our future.

If ever robots rise in revolution,
if ever they attack the human race,
at least you refrigerators won't be
amongst the ones to break the peace.

For you are the house-dog of machinery
a faithful and contented animal;
so give your door a docile wag for Man,
your living friend, and show him how you smile.

---

[1]**domination**   rule

The Inside of Things

by Brian Patten

Inside the dandelion seed is a clock,
Inside the egg is a chicken farm;
Inside a fist an army awaits,
Inside a kiss is an open palm.

Inside a snowflake an avalanche
Trembles and waits to get free;
Inside a raindrop a river plots
The best way to run to the sea.

The Seed Shop
by Muriel Stuart

Here in a quiet and dusty room they lie,
Faded as crumbled stone or shifting sand,
Forlorn as ashes, shrivelled, scentless, dry –
Meadows and gardens running through my hand.

In this brown husk[1] a dale[2] of hawthorn dreams,
A cedar in this narrow cell is thrust,
That will drink deeply of a century's streams,
These lilies shall make summer on my dust.

Here in their safe and simple house of death,
Sealed in their shells a million roses leap;
Here I can blow a garden with my breath,
And in my hand a forest lies asleep.

---

[1]**husk**   seed shell
[2]**dale**   valley

Gunpowder Plot

by Vernon Scannell

For days these curious cardboard buds have lain
In brightly coloured boxes. Soon the night
Will come. We pray there'll be no sullen rain
To make these magic orchids flame less bright.

Now in the garden's darkness they begin
To flower: the frenzied whizz of Catherine-wheel
Puts forth its fiery petals and the thin
Rocket roars to burst upon the steel

Bulwark[1] of a cloud. And then the guy,
Absurdly human phoenix, is again
Gulped by greedy flames: the harvest sky
Is flecked with threshed and glittering golden grain.

'Uncle! A cannon! Watch me as I light it!'
The women helter-skelter, squealing high,
Retreat; the paper-fuse is quickly lit,
A cat-like hiss and spit of fire, and sly

Falter, then the air is shocked with blast.
The cannon bangs and in my nostrils drifts
A bitter scent that brings the lurking past
Lurching to my side. The present shifts,

Allows a ten-year memory to walk
Unhindered now; and so I'm forced to hear
The banshee[2] howl of mortar and the talk
Of men who died; am forced to taste my fear.

---

[1] **bulwark**   defensive barrier
[2] **banshee**   mythical spirit woman said to howl when a death approaches

I listen for a moment to the guns,
The torn earth's grunts, recalling how I prayed.
The past retreats. I hear a corpse's sons –
'Who's scared of bangers!' 'Uncle John's afraid!'

'They'

by Siegfried Sassoon

The Bishop tells us: 'When the boys come back
They will not be the same; for they'll have fought
In a just cause: they lead the last attack
On Anti-Christ;[1] their comrades' blood has bought
New right to breed an honourable race.
They have challenged Death and dared him face to face.'

'We're none of us the same!' the boys reply.
'For George lost both his legs; and Bill's stone blind;
Poor Jim's shot through the lungs and like to die;
And Bert's gone syphilitic:[2] you'll not find
A chap who's served that hasn't found *some* change.'
And the Bishop said: 'The ways of God are strange!'

---

[1]**Anti-Christ**   Satan
[2]**syphilitic**   suffering from a sexually transmitted disease

Activities

On My Short-Sightedness

1 This poem's title is *On My Short-Sightedness*, but is it really about eye-sight? Discuss with a partner what else the poet might be writing about.

The Blind Man at the Fair

1 Read the poem out loud. Can you identify a sound that echoes throughout the poem? With a partner, discuss what, if anything, this repeated sound adds to the meaning of the poem. Share your thoughts with the class.

2 **a** Who do you think 'the blind man at the fair' really is? Re-read the poem carefully, then think about these questions and jot down your thoughts:
   ● How do you imagine the man? What is his age? appearance? job? Does he have a family? How does he move? How does he interact with other people?
   ● How did he become blind? Did he have an accident? an illness? Was he born blind?
   ● What is the setting of the poem? What period is it set in? What kind of environment is being described?

   b Use your notes to write a character sketch of about 200–300 words describing the man.

The Blind Boy

1 **a** Read the poem out loud. Can you identify a pattern to the rhymes? What effect does this have as you read or listen?

   b Which of the following words do you think best describe the poem's rhythm?

   jaunty   sad   slow   gloomy   bright   skipping   plodding

   c With a partner, discuss how the rhymes and rhythm help to create an identity for the blind boy and a mood for the poem.

First Sight

1   Imagine you were born in a very hot or a very cold country. You have just seen snow / felt the baking heat for the first time. Write a descriptive paragraph about your emotions and sensations at that moment.

Hares at Play

1   **a**   Have you ever seen a hare? If so, tell your classmates about it. Where was it? How would you describe the animal? If not, discuss what you know about hares. Do you know any stories about hares?

   b   Find examples of how the poet shows us the behaviour of the 'playing' hares. Look carefully at:
   • the particular words chosen to describe the hare's actions
   • the use of punctuation, especially in line 10
   • the repetition of words.

2   Think about another night-time creature such as an owl or a bat. Write a short poem about it. Try to create a sense of the animal's movements and behaviour.

Kob Antelope

1   This poem includes precise descriptions of the Kob antelope. Re-read the poem carefully and draw a picture of the animal. Label your picture with short quotations from the poem.

2   'A creature to pet and spoil / like a child.' This poem contains several similes (a simile compares one thing to something else using the word 'like' or the word 'as').

   a   Working with a partner, find as many similes in the poem as you can.

   b   Discuss how the similes help you to understand what the antelope is like. Think of three adjectives (that are not used in the poem) to describe the animal.

Mountain Lion

1 In a small group, prepare a dramatic reading of the poem. Follow
   these steps:
   - First read the poem aloud. Try to get a 'feel' for the poem's
     sounds and rhythms.
   - Divide the poem up into appropriate sections.
   - Decide how you will create different effects during your read-
     ing. Which lines will be read by individuals and which by the
     whole group? Which lines will be read quietly and which loud?
     What feelings will you try to convey at different moments in the
     poem?

   Perform your reading for the class.

2 How would you describe the atmosphere of *Mountain Lion*? Make a
   list of up to 10 words or phrases that help to create the poem's
   atmosphere. Next to each of your chosen words or phrases, make
   a short note explaining how it helps to create atmosphere.

Red Kites Rising

1 Why do you think this poem has been set out in this unusual
   shape? It might help you to think about the two parts of the poem:
   - What is each part about?
   - Can you find any contrasts between the two parts?

   Discuss your thoughts with a partner.

2 The poem ends with the phrase 'a force that looks for all the world /
   like ease.' What do you think the poet is saying about the red kites
   here? Write a short paragraph to sum up what you think the poem
   is about.

The Fly

1 Working with a partner, re-read the poem and discuss whether you
   agree with each of the following statements. Give reasons for your
   decisions.
   - The speaker in the poem feels that humans and flies are similar.
   - The speaker in the poem feels guilty.
   - The poem is depressing.

2   Some of William Blake's poems use very simple language and have
    been compared to nursery rhymes.
    a   Create a table to show any similarities you notice between *The
        Fly* and nursery rhymes or other poems for very young children
        that you know.
    b   Do you feel that the simple form and language used in this
        poem are suited to the subject matter? Discuss your views with
        your partner.

Acts of God

1   Poems often include a change of mood or atmosphere. Can you
    find a 'turning point' of this kind in this poem?
    a   Discuss in a small group how the two parts of the poem
        (before and after the turning point) differ.
    b   What words would your group use to describe the feelings of
        the speaker in the first and second parts of the poem? Make a
        list.

2   Imagine or think back to a time when you were frightened at night.
    Write a short poem about the experience. Think about:
    ● the noises you heard
    ● the effect of the darkness (for example, did it make your house
      seem bigger or unfamiliar, or create strange shadows in cor-
      ners?)
    ● your reactions to the situation.

Mawu of the Waters

1   'I fling oceans around me like a shawl.' 'I' in this poem is Mawu of
    the Waters – but who is Mawu? Discuss your thoughts in a small
    group or as a class.

2   Write your own poem in the style of *Mawu of the Waters*. Choose one
    of the following titles, or think of your own:
    ● Mawu of the forests
    ● Mawu of the snow and ice.

The Ferryboat and the Traveller

1 Some poems and stories are known as allegories. In an allegory, characters, objects or actions are often used as symbols for other things or ideas.

  a Do you think that this poem can be read as an allegory? If so, who or what is symbolised by the ferryboat and the traveller?

  b What do you feel the poet gains by using symbols in this poem? Do you find this approach effective?

  Discuss your ideas in a small group.

The Fridge

1 If a fridge were a person, what kind of person would it be? Discuss and compare your thoughts with a partner.

2 a Choose a household object or piece of machinery to write about as if it were a person. First organise your thoughts using a spider diagram. Be as imaginative as you can. Think about:
   ● who your object would be (for example, an antique chair might be 'an ageing old man with creaking bones')
   ● how your object would move and behave.

   b Write a short poem or a paragraph of prose to describe your object as if it were a person. You could keep the identity of your object secret. Then swap your writing with a partner – can you guess what object each other has written about?

The Inside of Things

1 Read the poem with a partner. Working together, write some more verses for the poem. The following lines might help you get started:
   ● Inside a grain of wheat . . .
   ● Inside a shout . . .
   ● Inside a handshake . . .

   Share your work with another pair.

The Seed Shop

1 **a** This poem is full of contrasts. Make two lists: one of the words in the poem that you associate with death; the other of words that you associate with life.

   b Write a sentence or two to summarise your understanding of the poem, and comment on how the contrasting language helps to get across the poem's meaning.

Gunpowder Plot

1 The poet, Vernon Scannell, fought and was injured in World War II. Discuss the following questions with a partner:

   a How has Scannell captured the feelings of someone who has experienced war in this poem?

   b Is it 'only' fear that Uncle John feels, or are his feelings more complex? Can you identify particular words or images that suggest what his feelings might be?

2 Imagine you are Uncle John and have just heard your nephews say 'Uncle John's afraid!'. Write a letter to them explaining your response to the fireworks display. Think about:

   • what you can and can't tell them about the horrors of war
   • whether you will mention their father
   • the tone of the letter (for example, will it be angry? calm?).

'They'

1 Discuss the following questions in a small group.

   a Almost all of the first verse of this poem is a statement by 'the Bishop'. He says that 'the boys . . . will not be the same'. What do you think he means by this?

   b How would you describe the Bishop's attitude towards the dead and wounded and the war in general? Compare this to the attitudes of 'the boys' who speak in the poem's second verse.

   c Look at the structure of the poem. What contrasts do you notice between the verses? Does the poem's structure help the reader to understand what the poet is saying?

   d Why do you think the poet chose the title 'They' for this poem?

Compare and contrast

1   Working with a partner, imagine a conversation about blindness between the blind boy and the blind man at the fair. What would each character say? How would they react to one another? Script a short conversation between the two characters, then act it out. You could perform it for the class.

2   Several of the poems in this section give us a 'view' of a particular animal. Choose two or three of the poems featuring animals and make notes on the different ways in which the poets help us to 'see' the animals they are describing.

Draw up a table like the one below to help you structure your notes. One or two ideas have been included to start you off.

	Hares at Play		Kob Antelope	
	Quote	How this helps us 'see' the animal	Quote	How this helps us 'see' the animal
Interesting or unusual word choice	'dance and play'	Poet describes hare in human terms. Helps to suggest lively and carefree movements – contrasts with animal's fear in morning.		
Figurative language (metaphors and similes)			'The head / beautiful like carved wood.'	Comparison with desirable object suggests vulnerability? Does this put antelope at risk?
Rhythms and sounds				
Use of punctuation				
Other				

3   Both *The Seed Shop* and *The Inside of Things* include ways of looking at or thinking about common, everyday things in a new or unusual way. Write a short essay to explore the similarities and differences between the two poems. Pay close attention to:
   ● each poet's choice of words
   ● the form of each poem
   ● the repeated sounds and rhythms in each poem.

Does one poem make a stronger impression on you than the other? Explain your view, making sure to include quotations from both poems to support your opinions.

4   *Gunpowder Plot* and *'They'* both address the issue of war; both were written by men with personal experience of warfare.
   a   In a small group, research Scannell's and Sassoon's involvement in war. Try to find out:
      ● which wars they fought in
      ● what happened to them in wartime
      ● their attitudes to the wars they fought in.

   b   Re-read both poems. How would you describe the attitude towards war that each poem presents? Find quotations to support your view.

   c   Working in a small group, use your research findings and your notes on both poems to create a presentation for your class.

5   The form of a poem can sometimes contribute to its meaning. Choose two or more poems from this section whose forms help the reader to understand what the poems are about. Write two or three paragraphs to explain how the poets' chosen forms help convey meaning.

2 You and me

The poems in this section are about being separate individuals, with our hopes, fears and needs, and about how we get on with other people. As young people we are especially concerned with who we are, and how we can relate to others. We have our heroes, as in Benjamin Zephaniah's *Heroes*; we develop friendships, as in *Shocks*; and sometimes we try to impress, as in *Sewing Fingertips*.

There can also be challenges in relationships, and some of the poems here are about the strange behaviour of the opposite sex, or our parents. Others are about what happens when we lose touch with people, or with our childhood selves. Three more serious poems, *The Shout*, *The Apple-Raid* and *Mid-Term Break* are about death.

Activities

1 In many of the poems in this section, poets recall key moments in their childhood (e.g. *Footings*). Think of two or three things that happened to you when you were younger and that had a lasting influence on you. Share your experiences with a partner. Your memories might include:

   • events that led you to be scared of something such as the dark, or bees
   • the behaviour of someone that you wanted to emulate or that made you determined never to behave that way yourself
   • a change in circumstances, such as moving home or school, or losing a loved one.

2 Many of the poems in the section are about friendships. Discuss, in a small group or as a class, friends you had when you were younger, and the things you remember doing with them. Are you still friends with these people? How are your friendships now different from those you had when you were much younger?

3 Think about what makes the people in your life special to you. Are the people you care about people that you always get on with? Do they all share the same interests as you?

Choose three key people in your life – these might include a parent, a sibling, a friend, a teacher or even a pop-star or actor you really admire. Write a paragraph about your relationship with each person you have chosen, remembering to say why they are a special part of your life.

One

by James Berry

Only one of me
and nobody can get a second one
from a photocopy machine.

Nobody has the fingerprints I have.
Nobody can cry my tears, or laugh my laugh
or have my expectancy when I wait.

But anybody can mimic my dance with my dog.
Anybody can howl how I sing out of tune.
And mirrors can show me multiplied
many times, say, dressed up in red
or dressed up in grey.

Nobody can get into my clothes for me
or feel my fall for me, or do my running.
Nobody hears my music for me, either.

I am just this one.
Nobody else makes the words
I shape with sound, when I talk.

But anybody can act how I stutter in a rage.
Anbody can copy echoes I make.
And mirrors can show me multiplied
many times, say, dressed up in green
or dressed up in blue.

Friendship

by Cole Porter

If you're ever in a jam,
    Here I am.
If you're ever in a mess,
    S.O.S.
If you ever feel so happy you land in jail,
    I'm your bail.[1]

It's friendship, friendship,
Just a perfect blendship.
When other friendships have been forgot,
Ours will still be hot.

If you're ever up a tree,
    Phone to me.
If you're ever down a well,
    Ring my bell.
If you ever lose your teeth and you're out to dine,
    Borrow mine.

It's friendship, friendship,
Just a perfect blendship.
When other friendships have been forgate,
Ours will still be great.

If they ever black your eyes,
    Put me wise.
If they ever cook your goose,
    Turn me loose.
If they ever put a bullet through your brain,
    I'll complain.

---

[1]**bail**   money paid to get someone out of prison while awaiting trial

It's friendship, friendship,
Just a perfect blendship.
When other friendships have been forgit,
Ours will still be it.

Friendship

by Elizabeth Jennings

Such love I cannot analyse;
It does not rest in lips or eyes,
Neither in kisses nor caress.
Partly, I know, it's gentleness

And understanding in one word
Or in brief letters. It's preserved
By trust and by respect and awe.
These are the words I'm feeling for.

Two people, yes, two lasting friends.
The giving comes, the taking ends.
There is no measure for such things.
For this all Nature slows and sings.

Heroes

by Benjamin Zephaniah

Heroes are funny people, dey are lost an found
Sum heroes are brainy an sum are muscle-bound,
Plenty heroes die poor an are heroes after dying
Sum heroes mek yu smile when yu feel like crying.
Sum heroes are made heroes as a political trick
Sum heroes are sensible an sum are very thick!
Sum heroes are not heroes cause dey do not play de game
A hero can be young or old and have a silly name.
Drunks an sober types alike hav heroes of dere kind
Most heroes are heroes out of sight an out of mind,
Sum heroes shine a light upon a place where darkness fell
Yu could be a hero soon, yes, yu can never tell.
So if yu see a hero, better treat dem wid respect
Poets an painters say heroes are a prime subject,
Most people hav heroes even though some don't admit
I say we're all heroes if we do our little bit.

These I Have Loved

by Rupert Brooke

These I have loved:
                  White plates and cups, clean-gleaming,
Ringed with blue lines; and feathery, faery dust;
Wet roofs, beneath the lamp-light; the strong crust
Of friendly bread; and many-tasting food;
Rainbows; and the blue bitter smoke of wood;
And radiant raindrops couching in cool flowers;
And flowers themselves, that sway through sunny hours,
Dreaming of moths that drink under the moon;
Then, the cool kindliness of sheets, that soon
Smooth away trouble; and the rough male kiss
Of blankets; grainy wood; live hair that is
Shining and free; blue-massing clouds; the keen
Unpassioned beauty of a great machine;
The benison[1] of hot water; furs to touch;
The good smell of old clothes; and other such –
The comfortable smell of friendly fingers,
Hair's fragrance, and the musty reek[2] that lingers
About dead leaves and last year's ferns . . .

                      (Extract from 'The Great Lover')

---

[1]**benison**   blessing
[2]**musty reek**   damp, stale smell

Unburglars

by Philip Gross

When we came down and found the back door open
first it was the dash from room to room – *video?*

stereo? TV? then the private hiding places. All
intact: relief, laced with a rather eager gratitude

like being let off with a caution. Till that night,
tucked down again, every catch and bolt piously[1]

checked, that's when it came in with the calm assurance
of a curse. They *had* been. Come and seen, moved through

the house, hardly stirring the dust on the carpet, taking
it all in. Peeling gloves on like a surgeon's: to them,

a fingerprint would be as gross as skid-marks. And
no need to take a thing – why, when they have it all

and need so little? Little breaths: if they'd bent over you
sleeping (when you could still sleep) how would you know?

---

[1]**piously**   as if following religious rules

Boy at the Window

by Richard Wilbur

Seeing the snowman standing all alone
In dusk and cold is more than he can bear.
The small boy weeps to hear the wind prepare
A night of gnashings[1] and enormous moan.
His tearful sight can hardly reach to where
The pale-faced figure with bitumen[2] eyes
Returns him such a god-forsaken stare
As outcast Adam gave to Paradise.[3]

The man of snow is, nonetheless, content,
Having no wish to go inside and die.
Still, he is moved to see the youngster cry.
Though frozen water is his element,
He melts enough to drop from one soft eye
A trickle of the purest rain, a tear
For the child at the bright pane surrounded by
Such warmth, such light, such love, and so much fear.

---

[1]**gnashings**   grinding of teeth
[2]**bitumen**   tar (black)
[3]**Paradise**   Garden of Eden

Footings

by Colette Bryce

You could see, for the life of you, no clear point
in monkeying around, seven feet to the ground;
to slide from the belly, swing there (caught
by the arms, by the palms, by the fingertips), drop.
If I'd taken the trouble of minuses, pluses,
the length of the body, the height of the wall,
even pushed myself to prediction, scared you;
as it stood, before you leapt, I dared you.

And the lane in was yeared[1] into two deep tracks
as we found our feet in the lengthened light,
for those with the leap approach to life,
for those who measure, look, think twice.
Both of us sobbing, I shouldered you home
with your hard-won knowledge, broken bone.

---

[1]yeared   stretched out in the paths of years to come

Purge

by Sheila Glen Bishop

We didn't like Doll much.
She had real ringlets once,
but snipped too often, now
just tufts . . . her eyes
looked sideways – sly – meant
to be cute. I held her up-side-
-down by grubby petticoats.
Oh, she deserved to die, alright
– and we were looking for a victim!

Let's do it now, you said.

After all, that's what they did
to Joan of Arc[1] – and lots of others.
History says so . . . It purged
the demons out and saved their souls
(straightened their sideways eyes, perhaps?)
in one tremendous flame!
Fun, too . . .

We'll need a stake, you said.

Unholy glee possessed us as
we tied her to it, scrunched
old newspaper and twigs under
her stupid feet. You pinched
the matches, I arranged the hands
pretending prayer (we couldn't
find a crucifix) stood back,
savoured the moment when the fire
frizzled her skirts and what remained
of all her hair.

---

[1]**Joan of Arc** French saint burnt at the stake

Whizzo!

But legs and body still refused
to burn. Just scorched, exuded
coils of slug-glue stuffing – horrid
and irreparable. The eyes
still ogled[2] . . .

                        Sickened,
we turned away, and stung with smoke
or shame, our own eyes met then
slid away again – silently,
sideways, sly – like Doll's had been.

She can't have suffered much, you said.

---

[2]**ogled**   stared

Sewing Fingertips

by Jean Sprackland

Queuing at Miss Pope's desk
to have our cross-stitch checked,
we made daring needlework of our fingers
in moss green and golden brown.
More thrilling than those woven squares
where you followed the holes,
no piercing involved.

We were desperadoes, raising the stakes
by sewing ourselves to our jumpers,
to the pages of our jotters,
to each other.

Like firewalkers, or sleepers on beds of nails,
we vied[1] and swaggered:[2]
see my magic,
look how brave I am,
I never make a fuss.

Except the new girl,
weeping through clenched teeth,
hand embroidered with blood.
Learning what it means
to try too hard.

---

[1]**vied**   competed
[2]**swaggered**   showed off, boasted

Shocks

by Jean Sprackland

Remember those first thrills, the charge
that went cracking through you?
Sunday afternoons we went out on our bikes,
me and next-door Julie.
She had black ringlets and a wicked smile.

We crossed the dual carriageway
like small determined animals swimming a swollen river.
Then out into the lanes. A dappled horse
shambled hopefully towards the gate.
We dropped our bikes on the verge,
took out apple cores and polo mints.
We pretended this was why we'd come.
We perched on the gate,
picking scabs of rust and telling secrets:
the time Derek Wesley saw a dead man
in the old air-raid shelter. The little packets
Julie found in her dad's wardrobe.

She always made the first move,
casual and bold by the electric fence.
She bet me anything it wasn't on.
Touch it. I dare you. I said it first.
The blood jittered in my fingertips,
my throat. I thought I could hear the current
singing in the cable. I reached out.

Tell Your Mother I Saved Your Life

by Jean Sprackland

At the top of the stairs in the Science Block
you're shoved then grabbed back by your blazer.
The world tilts, your veins fizz.
Some boy and his goofy mates cackle behind you.
It's just a laugh, don't you get it?

This foreshadows new mysteries with boys
at parties or bus stops. You are forever guessing,
wrong-footed, checking the shadows
for his sniggering gang. He says something
which could mean this or that. He keeps not kissing you
then just as your bus arrives he changes his mind,
and you falter again at the top of that stairwell,
possessed, vertiginous.[1] You sit at the back,
your head throbbing against the misted glass.

---

[1]**vertiginous**   dizzy with height

Smothering Sunday

by John Hegley

To a wonderful mother
with wrinkly skin,
this card was concocted[1]
by one of your kin.
I hope that you like it
it's specially for you,
I've sprinkled some glitter
on top of some glue.
I don't like the bought ones
I thought you should know,
they're too superficial[2]
and two quid a throw[3]
some of them.

---

[1]**concocted** made up
[2]**superficial** shallow
[3]**a throw** each

Bringing Up a Single Parent

by Brian Patten

It's tough bringing up a single parent.
They get really annoyed when they can't stay out late,
or when you complain about them acting soppy
over some nerdy new friend,
(even though you are doing it for their own good).
It's exhausting sometimes, the way you have to please them,
and do things you absolutely hate while pretending
it's exactly what you want.
Yep. Bringing up a single parent
is a real chore.
You don't get extra pocket money for them,
or special grants,
and you have to get up in the morning
and allow them to take you to school
so they can boast to their friends
about how clever you are.
And what's worse,
you have to allow them to fret over you,
otherwise they get terribly worried.
And if you're out doing something interesting after school
you have to keep popping home all the time
to check they're not getting up to any mischief
with a new friend, or smoking, or drinking too much.

You have to try and give single parents
that extra bit of attention.
But once you've got them trained,
with a bit of patience and fortitude
they're relatively easy to look after.
Still, it can be tough
bringing up a single parent.

In the Playground

by Michael Rosen

In the playground
at the back of our house
there have been some changes.

They said:
the climbing frame's not safe
So they sawed it down.

They said:
the paddling pool's not safe
so they drained it dry.

They said:
the see-saw's not safe
so they took it away.

They said:
the sand pit's not safe
so they fenced it in.

They said:
the playground's not safe
so they locked it up.

sawn down
drained dry
taken away
fenced in
locked up.

How do you feel?
Safe?

Conkers

by Grace Nichols

Autumn treasures
from the horsechestnut tree

Lying roly poly
among their split green casings

Shiny and hard
like pops of polished mahogany[1]

An English schoolboy
picking them up –

The same compulsive
fickle[2] avidity[3] –

As I picked up
orange-coloured cockles

Way back then
from a tropical childhood tree

Hand about to close in . . .
then spotting another even better

Now, waiting on our bus
we grown-ups watch him

---

[1]**mahogany**   a hard, dark wood
[2]**fickle**   changing one's mind
[3]**avidity**   eagerness, greed

Not knowing how or why
we've lost our instinct

For gathering
the magic shed of trees

Though in partyful mood
in wineful spirits

We dance around crying,
'Give me back my conker.'

The Shout

by Simon Armitage

We went out
into the school yard together, me and the boy
whose name and face

I don't remember. We were testing the range
of the human voice:
he had to shout for all he was worth,

I had to raise an arm
from across the divide to signal back
that the sound had carried.

He called from over the park – I lifted an arm.
Out of bounds,
he yelled from the end of the road,

from the foot of the hill,
from beyond the look-out post of Fretwell's Farm –
I lifted an arm.

He left town, went on to be twenty years dead
with a gunshot hole
in the roof of his mouth, in Western Australia.

Boy with the name and face I don't remember,
you can stop shouting now, I can still hear you.

The Apple-Raid

by Vernon Scannell

Darkness came early, though not yet cold:
Stars were strung on the telegraph wires;[1]
Street lamps spilled pools of liquid gold;
The breeze was spiced with garden fires.

That smell of burnt leaves, the early dark.
Can still excite me but not as it did
So long ago when we met in the park –
Myself, John Peters and David Kidd.

We moved out of town to the district where
The lucky and wealthy had their homes
With garages, gardens, and apples to spare
Clustered in the trees' green domes.

We chose the place we meant to plunder[2]
And climbed the wall and tip-toed through
The secret dark. Apples crunched under
Our feet as we moved through the grass and dew.

We found the lower boughs of a tree
That were easy to reach. We stored the fruit
In pockets and jerseys until all three
Boys were heavy with their tasty loot.

---

[1]**telegraph wires**   telephone wires
[2]**plunder**   rob

Safe on the other side of the wall
We moved back to town and munched as we went.
I wonder if David remembers at all
That little adventure, the apples' fresh scent.

Strange to think that he's fifty years old.
That tough little boy with scabs on his knees;
Stranger to think that John Peters lies cold
In an orchard in France beneath apple trees.

Geography Lesson
by Brian Patten

Our teacher told us one day he would leave
And sail across a warm blue sea
To places he had only known from maps,
And all his life had longed to be.

The house he lived in was narrow and grey
But in his mind's eye he could see
Sweet-scented jasmine clinging to the walls,
And green leaves burning on an orange tree.

He spoke of the lands he longed to visit,
Where it was never drab or cold.
I couldn't understand why he never left,
And shook off the school's stranglehold.

Then halfway through his final term
He took ill and never returned.
He never got to that place on the map
Where the green leaves of the orange trees burned.

The maps were redrawn on the classroom wall;
His name forgotten, he faded away.
But a lesson he never knew he taught
Is with me to this day.

I travel to where the green leaves burn,
To where the ocean's glass-clear and blue
To places our teacher taught me to love –
And which he never knew.

Mid-Term Break

by Seamus Heaney

I sat all morning in the college sick bay
Counting bells knelling[1] classes to a close,
At two o'clock our neighbours drove me home.

In the porch I met my father crying –
He had always taken funerals in his stride –
And Big Jim Evans saying it was a hard blow.

The baby cooed and laughed and rocked the pram
When I came in, and I was embarrassed
By old men standing up to shake my hand

And tell me they were 'sorry for my trouble'.
At ten o'clock an ambulance arrived
With the corpse, stanched[2] and bandaged by nurses.

Next morning I went up into the room. Snowdrops
And candles soothed the bedside; I saw him
For the first time in six weeks. Paler now,

Wearing a poppy bruise on his left temple,
He lay in the four-foot box as in his cot.
No gaudy scars, the bumper knocked him clear.

A four foot box, a foot for every year.

---

[1]**knelling**   ringing
[2]**stanched**   (blood) flow stopped

Night Mail
by W. H. Auden

This is the night mail crossing the border,
Bringing the cheque and the postal order,
Letters for the rich, letters for the poor,
The shop at the corner and the girl next door,
Pulling up Beattock,[1] a steady climb –
The gradient's[2] against her but she's on time.

Past cotton grass and moorland boulder,
Shovelling white steam over her shoulder,
Snorting noisily as she passes
Silent miles of wind-bent grasses;
Birds turn their heads as she approaches,
Stare from the bushes at her blank-faced coaches;
Sheepdogs cannot turn her course
They slumber on with paws across,
In the farm she passes no one wakes
But a jug in the bedroom gently shakes.

Dawn freshens, the climb is done.
Down towards Glasgow she descends
Towards the steam tugs, yelping down the glade of cranes
Towards the fields of apparatus,[3] the furnaces
Set on the dark plain like gigantic chessmen.
All Scotland waits for her;
In the dark glens,[4] beside the pale-green sea lochs
Men long for news.

---

[1]**Beattock**   a hill in Scotland
[2]**gradient**   slope
[3]**apparatus**   machinery
[4]**glens**   wooded valleys

Letters of thanks, letters from banks,
Letters of joy from the girl and boy,
Receipted bills and invitations
To inspect new stock or visit relations,
And applications for situations,
And timid lovers' declarations,
And gossip, gossip from all the nations;
News circumstantial,[5] news financial,
Letters with holiday snaps to enlarge in
Letters with faces scrawled on the margin.
Letters from uncles, cousins and aunts,
Letters to Scotland from the South of France,
Letters of condolence to Highlands and Lowlands,
Notes from overseas to the Hebrides;
Written on paper of every hue
The pink, the violet, the white and the blue
The chatty, the catty, the boring, adoring,
The cold and official and the heart's outpouring,
Clever, stupid, short and long,
The typed and the printed and the spelt all wrong.

Thousands are still asleep
Dreaming of terrifying monsters
Or a friendly tea beside the band at Cranston's or Crawford's;
Asleep in working Glasgow, asleep in well-set Edinburgh,
Asleep in granite Aberdeen.
They continue their dreams
But shall wake soon and long for letters.
And none will hear the postman's knock
Without a quickening of the heart
For who can bear to feel himself forgotten?

---

[5]**circumstantial** to do with situations

Activities

One

1   This poem describes how certain characteristics of the poet could be imitated, but shows that essentially he is unique. Write your own poem, based on this one, about what makes you unique.

Friendship (Cole Porter)

1   This lyric is a mostly light-hearted list of promises about how the poet/singer will help his/her friend if he/she is in various kinds of trouble.

   a   Discuss in a small group which lines you like best and which are slightly less light-hearted.

   b   Think of other possible sorts of problem that could be included in the poem – come up with at least one idea each.

   c   Choose a problem each and make up a verse about it.

Friendship (Elizabeth Jennings)

1   The poem associates several abstract nouns (words for things you cannot experience) with your senses. Two examples are 'gentleness' and 'understanding'. Find three more in the second verse. Then make a mind map or similar diagram showing other qualities like this that you associate with friendship or look for in a friend.

2   Write two or three paragraphs about your views on friendship. Consider:

- what makes a good friend
- what friendship is
- how friendships change.

Heroes

1   a   In groups of four or five, divide the poem into sections and read it aloud, a section each, with a strong rap beat. Don't leave any pause between speakers.

   b   The poet spells some words to suggest a West Indian accent. Discuss how you think this affects the poem, and whether it works better read aloud than on the page.

2   Do any of your own heroes fit any of Benjamin Zephaniah's cat-
    egories? Write several paragraphs about one of your heroes,
    explaining why you admire him/her.

These I Have Loved

1   **a**   On a sheet of plain paper, draw symbols to represent each of
            the five senses: sight, hearing, touch, taste and smell. Scatter
            them around the page. Then choose phrases from the poem
            that especially appeal to each sense and copy them below the
            appropriate symbol. For example, the second line is visual: it
            appeals to the sense of sight.
    b   Which sense is unrepresented in the poem? Under the correct
            symbol, write a line of your own appealing to this sense.

2   Write your own poem about your favourite things. Make sure that
    it appeals to the senses.

Unburglars

1   What is the sequence of emotions that the poet and his partner go
    through, from when they find the back door open, to when they go
    to bed that night? With a partner, discuss and try to explain their
    emotions, focusing especially on why they feel cursed when noth-
    ing has been stolen.

2   Write a short paragraph for each of the following words and phrases.
    Explain its meaning and how it adds to the mood of the poem:
    a   *piously*
    b   *Peeling gloves on like a surgeon's*
    c   *as gross as skid-marks*

Boy at the Window

1   Jot down some notes in answer to the following questions.
    a   Which phrases in the first part of the poem especially show
            that the boy is worried about the snowman? How does alliter-
            ation (the repetition of consonant sounds) help to make his
            worries sound more intense?
    b   In what ways does the poet surprise us in the second part of the
            poem? How effective do you find his technique?

2 Draw the snowman with a large speech bubble containing the words that you think he might say to the boy if he could speak.

Footings

1 Discuss the poem with a partner. Use these questions to help you.

  a How does the first part of the poem express the more careful approach to getting down off a wall? (Think especially of the words in brackets, and of how the poet suggests using maths.)

  b The word 'yeared' suggests that this incident influences the two girls for all the years to come in their lives. Explain what two sorts of people are described and which sort you think each girl will become.

2 Which sort of person do you think you are? Write three paragraphs about whether you are you a 'looker' or a 'leaper'. Which is it better to be?

Purge

1 Working with a partner, carry out a hot-seating exercise to explore the following questions:

- What makes the children burn Doll?
- What religious references are there in the poem?
- Why do the children feel ashamed at the end of the poem?

Take it in turns to play one of the children and the interviewer.

Sewing Fingertips

1 Write a poem of your own about doing something to show off, as these girls seem to do. Include a comparison, as in 'Like firewalkers' and some boasts, as in *'look how brave I am'*.

Shocks

1 Find the one simile in the poem (a simile compares one thing to something else using the word 'like' or the word 'as'). Discuss with a partner why you think the poet uses it. See if you can think of an alternative.

2   Discuss with a partner why you think the girls come to touch the electric fence, and why they pretend this is not what they have come to do.

3   Either   Write a poem describing the experience from Julie's point of view. Try to express what sort of girl you think she is.

     Or   Imagine the horse can talk and write a poem from its point of view. Describe what it sees every Sunday afternoon.

Tell Your Mother I Saved Your Life

1   Discuss the following in a small group:
- The poem's title
- In what ways the girl narrating the poem finds that boys make her feel uncertain or confused, first in school, then later at parties and bus-stops.

2   Write your own short poem from a boy's point of view, describing what you/he might find difficult about girls.

3   Write two paragraphs about the different ways in which boys and girls tend to treat each other, and why.

Smothering Sunday

1   John Hegley is a performance poet. With a partner, read this poem aloud. What is the effect of the regular rhythm and rhyme? What is the effect of the last line breaking out of this set pattern?

2   Design a humorous card of your own. It could be a Mother's Day card, or a card for another important person in your life – a birthday card, for example, or a thank you card. Write an appropriate poem inside.

Bringing Up a Single Parent

1   In a small group, divide the poem up and read it aloud to bring out the ironic humour. Why is it funny?

2 Write a poem of your own that turns a relationship back to front in a similar way. Here are some suggestions:
   ● 'Training Your Owner' (by a dog, cat or other pet)
   ● 'It's Tough Having a New Teacher'
   Alternatively, write a short prose magazine article on your chosen subject.

In the Playground

1 Make brief notes in answer to these questions:
   a Who are 'they' in this poem?
   b What is the effect of the repeated 'They said' and 'so they'?
   c How do you think this reflects the poet's attitude to 'Health and Safety' issues and playgrounds?

2 Write a speech arguing that children's playgrounds should be made either more safe or more challenging.

Conkers

1 The poet sounds nostalgic and wistful, as if she misses something. In a group, explore what you think she is missing (it could be more than one thing!).

2 Imagine you are twenty years older than you are now, and living in a foreign country. What things might you miss? Write and illustrate a poem about one or more of these things.

The Shout

1 Discuss with a partner what is shocking about this poem. How does the poet manage to make it shocking? For example, does he use very vivid descriptive language?

2 The core message comes at the end of this poem. Brainstorm what you think this message is, using a mind map or spidergram. Then write an alternative last two lines expressing it in your own words.

The Apple-Raid

1 This poem is full of details and images that appeal to the senses in some way. Pick out the phrases from the poem that relate to each sense. What effect does this appeal to the senses have?

2 Discuss with a partner what is ironic about where John Peters is buried, and how this affects your feeling about the poem when you have finished reading it.

Geography Lesson

1 On a sheet of plain paper, draw images to capture the contrast between where the teacher lives and where he dreams of going. Use colour if possible. Under each image, write the phrase or line that suggests it.

2 Write a paragraph to sum up what lesson you think Brian Patten learned from his teacher. How would you personally put this lesson into action if you got the chance?

Mid-Term Break

1 Discuss in a small group:
   a   who Seamus Heaney is writing about
   b   what exactly has happened
   c   roughly how old Heaney was at the time of the event described.

2 This poem is partly about time passing. Find all the references to time in the poem and create a timeline or flow chart to show the stages described.

Night Mail

1 This poem has a very strong rhythm. Try tapping it out as you say the first few lines. How does it reflect the subject of the poem? Notice how the rhythm changes in the third verse.

2 In a small group or as a class, prepare a presentation of the poem. One option is for one or more pupils to mime actions for some of the lines. You could even learn at least part of the poem off by heart.

Compare and contrast

1   The two poems that share the title *Friendship* are very different. The poem by Elizabeth Jennings gives no actual examples of friendship. Instead, it talks about friendship in a general way. How does this compare with Cole Porter's poem? Which approach do you prefer, and why?

2   *Footings*, *Sewing Fingertips* and *Shocks* all involve dares, and, to some extent, lessons.

   a   Create a table like the one below to compare how they do this:

	Footings	*Sewing Fingertips*	*Shocks*
Who is involved?			
What do they do?			
Why do they do it?			
What is the result?			

   b   Working in a small group, imagine a scene involving the characters from all three poems (e.g. in a school playground or park) where they discuss what they did in the poems. How might the characters interact? For example, will they exaggerate, try 'one-upmanship'?

   Work together to draft a script for the conversation. Take roles and perform a reading of your script for the rest of the class.

3   *The Shout*, *The Apple-Raid* and *Mid-Term Break* are all sadly shocking in their own ways. Compare the techniques used by the writers, then decide which poem you find saddest and why.

4   *Geography Lesson* and *Conkers* are both, in different ways, about loss, missing things, opportunities and far-off places. Write at least two paragraphs comparing how the two poems look at these different themes.

3 Out of doors

This section looks broadly at the world outside ourselves and our friends and family. *The Door* invites us to step outside and explore the waiting world of possibilities. Several poems look at our relationship with the animal world: how we use and abuse animals, as in *My Neighbours' Rabbit* and *My Mother Saw a Dancing Bear*, and how animals survive in a world dominated by human beings.

Other poems are about living outdoors, having no fixed address, and being exposed to the elements in fog or stormy weather. Some of the poems create a strong sense of atmosphere using striking imagery, as in *Slowly, the Fog, Mist* and *Feeding Out-Wintering Cattle at Twilight*.

Activities

1 Some of the poems in this section are about animals. Discuss your own attitude towards animals. For example:

 - Should human beings feel free to exploit animals in various ways?
 - Should we be vegetarian?
 - Do animals have rights?
 - Can animals teach us anything?
 - If you had to be an animal, what would you be?

2 Some of the poems in the section are about people living out-doors, without a permanent home. For each of the lifestyles below create a table that lists the advantages and disadvantages of living this way and at least one thing that you might miss about living at home.

 - Living permanently in a tent or caravan
 - Being a wanderer or traveller, with no fixed address
 - Being a homeless person living in a city

3 The following phrases are all taken from poems in this section:

- *the **hollow** wind* (from *The Door*)
- *Cape and sou'wester **streamed** / With rain as I rode to school* (from *The Bicycle*)
- *the wind's **swell**. The rain **like marbles*** (from *Caravan*)
- *the fog, / **Hunch-shouldered** with a **gray face*** (from *Slowly, the Fog*)
- *The **deft hands** of the morning mist* (from *Mist*)
- *the **wild** storm* (from *Trees in the Storm*)
- *The thunder will **take deep hold*** (from *Feeding Out-Wintering Cattle at Twilight*)

a Write your own description of a particular kind of weather. Include one or more of the phrases above.

b Look specifically at the words in bold in the phrases above. With a partner, discuss what effects and ideas the poets create by presenting different types of weather in these, sometimes unusual, ways.

The Door

by Miroslav Holub

Go and open the door.
  Maybe outside there's
  a tree, or a wood,
  a garden,
  or a magic city.

Go and open the door.
  Maybe a dog's rummaging.
  Maybe you'll see a face,
or an eye,
or the picture
  of a picture.

Go and open the door.
  If there's a fog
  it will clear.

Go and open the door.
  Even if there's only
  the darkness ticking,
  even if there's only
  the hollow wind,
  even if
    nothing
          is there,
go and open the door.

At least
there'll be
a draught.

Our Pond

by Daniel Pettiward

I am fond
Of our pond,
Of the superfine gloss
On its moss,
Its pink lilies and things
And the wings
Of its duck.

I am keen
On the green
Soupy surface of some
Of its scum,
Its water-waved weeds,
Its three reeds
And its muck.

Yesterday
As I lay
And admired its thick skin,
I fell in;
I went walloping down
Till I stuck.

I am fond
Of our pond,
But I like it much more
From the shore.
It was quite out of place
On my face,
Where it stuck.

My Neighbours' Rabbit

by Brian Patten

On the wall between my neighbours' garden and mine
a rabbit is sitting, shivering with cold.
They've been away some days now.
They've left out water and dry food
(though the rain's put paid to that).
What they haven't left behind is love.
They've asked no one to call in,
to stroke it, to make sure it's OK.
Having made it dependent upon them
they've abandoned it.
I take it from the wall,
feed it some apple, feel
how warm it grows, a furry volcano,
as warm as my absent neighbours are cold.
I marvel at how many sizes
the human heart comes in.
Some hearts have room inside them for a hutchful of rabbits,
some are so small
not even one rabbit would fit inside.
Perhaps my neighbours possess such hearts –
hearts that keep on shrinking,
that grow smaller and smaller until finally
nothing will fit inside, not even
the breath of a solitary rabbit.

My Mother Saw a Dancing Bear

by Charles Causley

My mother saw a dancing bear
By the schoolyard, a day in June.
The keeper stood with chain and bar
And whistle-pipe, and played a tune.

And bruin[1] lifted up its head
And lifted up its dusty feet,
And all the children laughed to see
It caper in the summer heat.

They watched as for the Queen it died.
They watched it march. They watched it halt.
They heard the keeper as he cried,
'Now, roly-poly!' 'Somersault!'

And then, my mother said, there came
The keeper with a begging-cup,
The bear with burning coat of fur,
Shaming the laughter to a stop.

They paid a penny for the dance,
But what they saw was not the show;
Only, in bruin's aching eyes,
Far-distant forests, and the snow.

---

[1]**bruin**   name for a bear

Hedgehog

by Anthony Thwaite

Twitching the leaves just where the drainpipe clogs
In ivy leaves and mud, a purposeful
Creature about its business. Dogs
Fear his stiff seriousness. He chews away

At beetles, worms, slugs, frogs. Can kill a hen
With one snap of his jaws, can taunt a snake
To death on muscled spines. Old countrymen
Tell tales of hedgehogs sucking a cow dry.

But this one, cramped by houses, fences, walls,
Must have slept here all winter in that heap
Of compost, or have inched by intervals
Through tidy gardens to this ivy bed.

And here, dim-eyed, but ears so sensitive
A voice within the house can make him freeze,
He scuffs the edge of danger, yet can live
Happily in our nights and absences.

A country creature, wary, quiet and shrewd,
He takes the milk we give him, when we're gone.
At night our slamming voices must sound crude
To one who sits and waits for silences.

Python

Traditional (*Nigeria*)

Swaggering[1] prince
giant among snakes.
They say python has no house.
I heard it a long time ago
and I laughed and laughed and laughed.
For who owns the ground under the lemon grass?
Who owns the ground under the elephant grass?
Who owns the swamp – father of rivers?
Who owns the stagnant[2] pool – father of waters?

Because they never walk hand in hand
people say that snakes only walk singly.
But just imagine
suppose the viper walks in front
the green mamba follows
and the python creeps rumbling behind –
who will be brave enough
to wait for them?

---

[1]**Swaggering**   showing off
[2]**stagnant**   stale

The Tomcat

by Don Marquis

At midnight in the alley
A tom-cat comes to wail,
And he chants the hate of a million years
As he swings his snaky tail.

Malevolent,[1] bony, brindled,[2]
Tiger and devil and bard,[3]
His eyes are coals from the middle of hell
And his heart is black and hard.

[1] **malevolent**   evil
[2] **brindled**   streaked
[3] **bard**   poet

He twists and crouches and capers[4]
And bares his curved sharp claws,
And he sings to the stars of the jungle nights
Ere cities were, or laws.

Beast from a world primeval,[5]
He and his leaping clan,
When the blotched red moon leers[6] over the roofs,
Give voice to their scorn of man.

He will lie on a rug tomorrow
And lick his silky fur,
And veil the brute in his yellow eyes,
And play he's tame, and purr.

But at midnight in the alley
He will crouch again and wail,
And beat the time for his demon's song
With the swing of his demon's tail.

---

[4]**capers**   dances about
[5]**primeval**   from the dawn of time
[6]**leers**   makes a nasty face

The Fox

by Phoebe Hesketh

It was twenty years ago I saw the fox
Gliding along the edge of prickling[1] corn,
A nefarious[2] shadow
Between the emerald field and bristling hedge,
On velvet feet he went.

The wind was kind, withheld from him my scent
Till my threaded gaze unmasked him standing there,
The colour of last year's beech leaves, pointed black,
Poised, uncertain, quivering nose aware
Of danger throbbing through each licking leaf.
One foot uplifted, balanced on the brink

Of perennial[3] fear, the hunter hunted stood.
I heard no alien stir in the friendly wood,
But the fox's sculpted[4] attitude was tense
With scenting, listening, with a seventh sense
Flaring to the alert; I heard no sound
Threaten the morning; and followed his amber stare,
But in that hair-breadth moment, that flick of the eye
He vanished.

And now, whenever I hear the expectant cry
Of hounds on the empty air,
I look to the gap in the hedge and see him there
Filling the space with fear; the trembling leaves
Are frozen in his stillness till I hear
His leashed-up breathing – how the stretch of time
Contracts within the flash of re-creation!

---

[1]**prickling**   just showing above ground
[2]**nefarious**   having a bad reputation
[3]**perennial**   lasting
[4]**sculpted**   still like a statue

An Old Woman of the Roads

by Pádraic Colum

O, to have a little house!
   To own the hearth and stool and all!
The heap'd-up sods[1] upon the fire,
   The pile of turf against the wall!

To have a clock with weights and chains
   And pendulum swinging up and down!
A dresser filled with shining delph,[2]
   Speckled and white and blue and brown!

I could be busy all the day
   Cleaning and sweeping hearth and floor;
And fixing on their shelf again
   My white and blue and speckled store!

I could be quiet there at night
   Beside the fire and by myself,
Sure of a bed and loth to leave
   The ticking clock and the shining delph!

Och! but I'm weary of mist and dark,
   And roads where there's never a house or bush,
And tired I am of bog and road,
   And the crying wind and the lonesome hush!

And I am praying to God on high,
   And I am praying Him night and day,
For a little house – a house of my own –
   Out of the wind's and the rain's way.

---

[1]**sods**   lumps of peat (a fuel)
[2]**delph**   china

Meg Merrilies

by John Keats

Old Meg she was a gipsy,
   And lived upon the moors;
Her bed it was the brown heath turf,
   And her house was out of doors.
Her apples were swart[1] blackberries,
   Her currants, pods o' broom;[2]
Her wine was dew of the wild white rose,
   Her book a churchyard tomb.

Her brothers were the craggy hills,
   Her sisters larchen trees;
Alone with her great family
   She lived as she did please.
No breakfast had she many a morn,
   No dinner many a noon,
And, 'stead of supper, she would stare
   Full hard against the moon.

But every morn, of woodbine[3] fresh
   She made her garlanding;
And, every night, the dark glen yew
   She wove, and she would sing.
And with her fingers, old and brown,
   She plaited mats of rushes,
And gave them to the cottagers
   She met among the bushes.

---

[1]**swart**   dark
[2]**broom**   a shrub that produces pods in summer; now know to be toxic
[3]**woodbine**   a trailing plant

Old Meg was brave as Margaret Queen,
    And tall as Amazon:[4]
An old red blanket cloak she wore,
    A chip-hat[5] had she on.
God rest her aged bones somewhere –
    She died full long agone!

---

[4]**Amazon**   mythical warrior woman
[5]**chip-hat**   hat made from chips of strips of wood

The Song of Wandering Aengus[1]

by W. B. Yeats

I went out to the hazel wood,
Because a fire was in my head,
And cut and peeled a hazel wand,
And hooked a berry to a thread;
And when white moths were on the wing,
And moth-like stars were flickering out,
I dropped the berry in a stream
And caught a little silver trout.

When I had laid it on the floor
I went to blow the fire aflame,
But something rustled on the floor,
And some one called me by my name:
It had become a glimmering girl
With apple blossom in her hair
Who called me by my name and ran
And faded through the brightening air.

Though I am old with wandering
Through hollow lands and hilly lands,
I will find out where she has gone,
And kiss her lips and take her hands;
And walk among long dappled grass,
And pluck till time and times are done
The silver apples of the moon,
The golden apples of the sun.

---

[1]**Aengus**   figure from Irish mythology, representing love, youth and poetic
    inspiration

Caravan

by Jean Sprackland

This is not about camels
bearing spices along a dusty contour
of the imagination, and sherbet,
and red and yellow silk

but a squarish sort of tin can
squat on the edge of a farmer's field:
nettles, stars, one cold tap.

Here you practise self-sufficiency
under a sheet-metal shelter;
assert a kind of integrity
via brown leatherette benches
which fold down into a bed;
calor gas; the neat double ring
where you cook a basic supper for two
and eat it all yourself.
You unfasten the plastic clip
and sit at the open window all day,
watching the sky lighten and darken,
the clouds part and regroup.

Let others go for something more upmarket:
thirty-six foot, six berth, cream with burgundy trim
and a name that means business –
The Challenger, The Marauder –
precision-parked on an exact pale
quota of grass like a slice of white bread,
at an intersection of rows and columns,
gravel paths and strimmed hedges,
with an electric hook-up, and neighbours.

There wouldn't be much to say:
Lovely morning. Keep it nice don't they.
And sometimes: *Quite a storm last night.*

Alone, you can let on
how much you like it:
the roll and sway of the van
on the wind's swell. The rain like marbles,
reassuring after all that silence.

The Bicycle

by Derek Mahon

There was a bicycle, a fine
Raleigh with five gears
And racing handlebars.
It stood at the front door
Begging to be mounted;
The frame shone in the sun.

I became like a character
In *The Third Policeman*,[1] half
Human, half bike, my life
A series of dips and ridges,
Happiness a free-wheeling
Past fragrant hawthorn hedges.

Cape and sou'wester[2] streamed
With rain as I rode to school
Side-tracking the bus routes.
Night after night I dreamed
Of valves, pumps, sprockets,[3]
Reflectors and repair kits.

Soon there were long rides
In the country, wet weekends
Playing cards in the kitchens
Of mountain youth hostels,
Day-runs to Monaghan,
Rough and exotic roads.

---

[1] *The Third Policeman*   novel by Irish author Brian O'Nolan
[2] **sou'wester**   rain hat
[3] **sprockets**   cogs turning a chain

It went with me to Dublin
Where I sold it the same winter;
But its wheels still sing
In the memory, stars that turn
About an eternal centre,
The bright spokes glittering.

Wind Gauge

by Gillian Clarke

At first barely discernible,[1]
a faint line drawn in graphite
on a water-marked page,
hairline crack in a bird's skull.

Then one evening to the west
where light dissolves in wind and water
another rises tall as sky
to finger prevailing westerlies.[2]

When the swallows come home
they'll ride the tangled currents
through webs of steel where once
was a wide aisle of air.

Once they raised stones,
cromlechs, megaliths,[3] as step by step
from winter's narrowest day
they counted home the sun.

Now they hoist masts,
steel circlets to crown a hill,
restless blades against the light
generating fire out of air.

---

[1]**discernible**   possible to see
[2]**prevailing westerlies**   winds which usually blow from west
[3]**cromlechs, megaliths**   prehistoric monuments

Slowly, the Fog

by F. R. McCreary

Slowly, the fog,
Hunch-shouldered with a gray face,
Arms wide, advances,
Finger-tips touching the way
Past the dark houses
And dark gardens of roses.
Up the short street from the harbour,
Slowly the fog,
Seeking, seeking;
Arms wide, shoulders hunched,
Searching, searching,
Out through the streets to the fields,
Slowly the fog –
A blind man hunting the moon.

Mist

by Douglas Gibson

Subtle as an illusionist[1]
The deft[2] hands of the morning mist
Play tricks upon my sight:
Haystacks dissolve and hedges lift
Out of the unseen fields and drift
Between the veils of white.

On the horizon, heads of trees
Swim with the mist about their knees,
And when the farm-dogs bark,
I turn to watch how on the calm
Of that white sea, the red-roofed farm
Floats like a Noah's Ark.

---

[1]**illusionist**   conjuror
[2]**deft**   quick and skilful

Trees in the Storm

by Brian Patten

The trees cling to the earth with tired fingers.
No matter how the sky tugs at them
they cling and cling.
They wrap their roots around the rabbit's warren,
the badger's holt, the mole's tunnel,
and cling and cling,
and won't let go no matter what.
They are afraid of being torn free and hurled,
root and branch, into the black soup of the sky.

Most things cling to the earth,
Most things that are not balloons
or birds or dandelion seeds,
or bits of paper or smoke,
or kites or clouds,
cling to the earth.
Even shadows cling to the earth.
Stones do it best,
they are the experts.

But among living things
it is the trees,
swaying and rattling their heads,
branches snapping like bones,
each dishevelled[1] twig wearing its necklaces of rain,
it is the trees
that fight so fiercely against the wild storm,
that cling and cling,
as if to life, as if never to give up.

---

[1]**dishevelled**   messed up, untidy

Feeding Out-Wintering Cattle at Twilight
by Ted Hughes

The wind is inside the hill.
The wood is a struggle – like a wood
Struggling through a wood. A panic
Only just holds off – every gust
Breaches[1] the sky-walls and it seems, this time,
The whole sea of air will pour through,
The thunder will take deep hold, roots
Will have to come out, every loose thing
Will have to lift and go. And the cows, dark lumps of dusk

---

[1]**breaches**   breaks through/over

Stand waiting, like nails in a tin roof.
For the crucial moment, taking the strain
In their stirring stillness. As if their hooves
Held their field in place, held the hill
To its trembling shape. Night-thickness
Purples in the turmoil, making
Everything more alarming. Unidentifiable, tiny
Birds go past like elf-bolts.[2]
Battling the hay-bales from me, the cows
Jostle and crush, like hulls[3] blown from their moorings
And piling at the jetty. The wind
Has got inside their wintry buffalo skins,
Their wild woolly bulk-heads,[4] their fierce, joyful breathings
And the reckless strength of their necks.
What do they care, their hooves
Are knee-deep in porage[5] of earth –
The hay blows luminous tatters from their chewings,
A fiery loss, frittering downwind,
Snatched away over the near edge
Where the world becomes water
Thundering like a flood-river at night.
They grunt happily, half-dissolved
On their steep, hurtling brink, as I flounder[6] back
Towards headlights.

---

[2]**elf-bolts**   lightning spears thrown by elves
[3]**hulls**   frames of ships
[4]**bulk-heads**   walls within the hulls of ships
[5]**porage**   porridge
[6]**flounder**   stagger

Activities

The Door

1 **a** In a small group, brainstorm what a door – and opening a door – could symbolise in this poem.

   b Then, using two sheets of paper or card, create a 'door' that can be opened to reveal the page beneath it. In the space representing 'outside the door', draw things to symbolise what might be outside your personal 'door'. For example, you might draw symbols of your hopes, such as a globe or plane to represent a hope to travel.

Our Pond

1 Working with a partner, to test how vivid a picture this poem creates, read it once, then cover it up and see if you can remember all the things the poet says he likes about the pond.

As you do so, notice if an image (perhaps including a colour) comes into your mind. Write down what you remember, then check the poem to see what you've missed.

2 This poem has a rhyme scheme that includes the whole poem, not just individual verses. Work out the rhyme scheme and discuss in your pairs how the use of enjambment (where a sentence or phrase continues from one line to the next) adds to its effect.

My Neighbours' Rabbit

1 Imagine the neighbours have come home and read Brian Patten's poem. Write their response to his criticism, either in prose or verse. You could include some of his phrases, such as the image of the 'furry volcano'.

My Mother Saw a Dancing Bear

1 Different countries have different views on animal rights. Working in a small group, look carefully at the poem and gather as many clues as you can about the characters mentioned. Make notes on what you discover.

2 Each person in the group should take on a role from the poem: these could include the narrator, the mother, someone from the crowd, the keeper and even the bear. One person will be the interviewer and will discover what each character was feeling before, during and after the bear's performance. Do they think what they saw was 'right'?

During the interview you could discuss:

• what the bear thinks of his keeper
• the 'Far-distant forests, and the snow'
• 'the summer heat'.

Try to make your interviews last between 5 and 7 minutes. Perform them for the rest of the class.

Hedgehog

1 a In a small group, discuss the essential qualities of the hedgehog, as described by Anthony Thwaite. Write down four or five qualities and support each with at least one word or phrase from the poem.

   b Referring to your evidence, write a single sentence that sums up all these qualities to describe the hedgehog.

Python

1 Discuss with a partner where this poem originated from and why it might have been written. How do you think the poem would have been performed; for example, would it have been read aloud or sung? Does the use of repetition in the poem affect your thoughts on this?

2 What message do you think the poet want to convey? Make notes about:

• the poet's attitude to pythons
• how this is expressed in each of the two parts of the poem.

3 Write a list of words used to describe the python. Then, think about how you feel about pythons and write a poem to express your feelings.

The Tomcat

1   This poem has a vigorous, musical rhythm to match the energy of its subject. Try beating out the rhythm. Then, divide it up among a small group and read it aloud, emphasising the rhythm.

What phrases especially suggest the cat's character? You could try to set the poem to music, turning it into a song with a melody that fits this character.

The Fox

1   Write down the phrases that suggest that the poet feels sympathetic towards the fox.

2   Hunting with dogs has been banned but many people would like to see it made legal again. Whatever your views, use phrases and ideas from the poem to write a defence of the fox. You could write this in verse or prose, in the third person or the first – as if you are the fox.

An Old Woman of the Roads

1   This dramatic monologue could be read as suggesting that we should be thankful for what we have. Do you agree with this interpretation? If not, why not? Discuss your ideas with a partner.

2   **a**   Discuss the following questions with a partner:
- What does the old woman find attractive in the idea of having a home?
- What is she weary of?

b   Write a paragraph discussing what you would find appealing or unappealing about the woman's wandering lifestyle.

Meg Merrilies

1   With a partner, discuss how Keats makes Meg's lifestyle sound attractive and how he expresses his admiration for her. Create a poster or pamphlet that promotes the benefits of Meg's lifestyle.

The Song of Wandering Aengus

1   Write a paragraph putting into your own words what seems to be the story of Wandering Aengus: how did he come to be a wanderer?

2   The poem is magically mysterious. Jot down the words and phrases that especially help to create this atmosphere.

Caravan

1   a   Make notes on how the poet emphasises that living in this caravan is not glamorous.

   b   How does she express her feelings about more upmarket caravans?

2   Imagine you spend a few days on your own in this caravan. Write a diary of your stay. Think about:
   •   how you will fill your time
   •   how the weather will affect your day
   •   what you might see as you stare out of the caravan window.

The Bicycle

1   Discuss with a partner why the poet finds such pleasure in riding the bicycle, and what phrases in the poem best express this.

2   Imagine that the poet is going to sell the bike. Write an advert for him to put in local shop windows. Use details from the poem as inspiration for any text or image you choose to include. The advert should fit on a postcard.

Wind Gauge

1   Gillian Clarke uses several metaphors (a metaphor describes one thing as if it were something else) in this poem to describe the wind gauges as they are erected off in the distance. Divide a page into two columns. In the left column, write down the metaphor; in the right, note what you think it suggests about how the poet sees the gauges.

Slowly, the Fog

1   This poem personifies fog (in personification, non-living objects are given human traits). Jot down any examples you find of personification in the poem. How does this technique make you respond to the fog? Think about how the poem uses repetition, and about its use of verbs: for example, 'advances' and 'Seeking, seeking'. Write a paragraph or two explaining how these techniques are used to build an atmosphere in the poem.

2   Choose another weather condition and give it human characteristics; for example, the sun might be happy and always optimistic. Turn your ideas into a short poem, in the style of *Slowly, the Fog*.

Mist

1   This poem uses a mixture of metaphors (e.g. 'deft hands') and similes (the first and last lines of the poem) to describe the mist. Working in a small group, find these images and discuss their effect.

Trees in the Storm

1   This poem is full of visual imagery (pictures). For example, find the references to 'tired fingers', 'black soup', and 'balloons'.

    Either   Write about the effect of some of these images and how they work together to make Brian Patten's point about trees.
    Or   Draw a picture including as many of these images as you can.

Feeding Out-Wintering Cattle at Twilight

1   Read the poem carefully, making sure that you understand its basic sense. Then, in a small group, discuss what lines or phrases express especially well:
    ● the wildness of the weather
    ● the solid strength of the cattle.

    Then, individually, choose your favourite phrase or line from those discussed, and present it to the class, explaining why you think it is so good.

Compare and contrast

1   *My Neighbours' Rabbit* and *My Mother Saw a Dancing Bear* are both about human treatment of animals. Write three paragraphs to compare them, looking at:
    - which animal is worse off, and why
    - what the poets' attitudes are towards the animals and their owners
    - which poem better expresses what life for that animal is like.

    Remember to use short quotations to illustrate your points. Finish by saying which poem you prefer, and why.

2   You have been asked to mount an advertising campaign to raise public awareness of, and sympathy for, either foxes or hedgehogs. You only have the budget to cover one. You can use phrases from either *Hedgehog* or *The Fox* in a campaign poster.

    To decide which to use, re-read the poems with a partner and compare how they create an overall picture of the animal. Use these questions to help you make a decision.
    - Which poem helps you to picture the animal more effectively?
    - Which conveys the animal's essential nature better?

    Design your poster.

3   *Python* and *The Tomcat* both describe animals that are 'wild' in different ways. Compare how the two poems express the power of the animal described. Which is more effective? Think about the following aspects:
    - imagery
    - choice of adjectives
    - repetition
    - use of rhythm and rhyme.

    Make notes on the two poems in the form of spidergrams, centring on pictures of the animals. Then write a short paragraph summing up which you think is the more effective.

4 *An Old Woman of the Roads* and *Meg Merrilies* both describe homeless women. With a partner, rehearse interviews with each of these two women to be presented on a TV programme of your choice. When you consider how the two women might respond to the interviewer's questions, be sure to take into account:

- their attitudes to their lifestyles, as conveyed in the poems
- the way in which the poets present the two women.

Try to devise at least four questions and answers for each woman.

5 You have been commissioned to make an atmospheric TV documentary about weather using lines from either *Trees in the Storm* or *Feeding Out-Wintering Cattle at Twilight.*

   a Make a table with two columns. In one column list all the images (similes and metaphors) which help create atmosphere in *Trees in the Storm*. In the second column, do the same for *Feeding Out-Wintering Cattle at Twilight*. Use your notes to help you choose which poem you think is most atmospheric, and which lines you will use in your documentary.

   b Make notes on what shots you will include to go with your chosen lines. To help you decide, answer these questions:

- What is the main focus of the poem?
- What details does the poem include?
- What mental pictures are created?

4 Ebb and flow

Stop and think for a moment about how things have changed in your life, and what things have stayed the same. This section is about change in all its forms – the ebb and flow of the sea, the rhythm of the seasons, and how a road through a wood can, over the years, be swallowed up by the trees, leaving only a ghostly memory. It is also about personal change, in growing up, as in *Dumbshow*, or never growing up, as in *Lucy Gray*, and the changes of war, as in the two poems by Thomas Hardy.

Activities

1 a Some of the poems in this section are about the sea. Think about your own feelings about the sea and what you associate with it. Make notes and create a mind map to show your ideas.

   b In a small group, discuss the different experiences of the sea that the different sorts of people listed below might have:

   - lifeboat men who rescue people in dangerous situations
   - fishermen
   - surfers
   - holiday-makers on Australian beaches
   - marine biologists
   - yacht sailors.

   c Individually, imagine you are one of these people. Prepare a talk describing your experience of the sea on one particular day.

2 Some of the poems are about death. In a small group, discuss what it is that you think makes poets want to write poems about death, and about related subjects, such as war. Why don't they just write about happy things?

3 You have time-travelled to 200 years in the future.

    a Make a list of things that have changed.

    b Plan a history lesson in which you introduce the students of the future to the early 21st century. What will you tell them in order to make them realise what life was like then? You could use your plan to give a short talk to your class, illustrated with real-life early 21st century objects.

The Sea

by James Reeves

The sea is a hungry dog,
Giant and grey.
He rolls on the beach all day.
With his clashing teeth and shaggy jaws
Hour upon hour he gnaws
The rumbling, tumbling stones,
And 'Bones, bones, bones, bones!'
The giant sea-dog moans,
Licking his greasy paws.

And when the night wind roars
And the moon rocks in the stormy cloud,
He bounds to his feet and snuffs and sniffs,
Shaking his wet sides over the cliffs,
And howls and hollos long and loud.

But on quiet days in May and June,
When even the grasses on the dune
Play no more their reedy tune,
With his head between his paws
He lies on the sandy shores,
So quiet, so quiet, he scarcely snores.

Sea Fever

by John Masefield

I must go down to the seas again, to the lonely sea and
    the sky,
And all I ask is a tall ship and a star to steer her by,
And the wheel's kick and the wind's song and the white
    sail's shaking,
And a grey mist on the sea's face, and a grey dawn
    breaking.

I must go down to the seas again, for the call of the
    running tide
Is a wild call and a clear call that may not be denied;
And all I ask is a windy day with the white clouds flying,
And the flung spray and the blown spume,¹ and the
    sea-gulls crying.

I must go down to the seas again, to the vagrant gypsy
    life,
To the gull's way and the whale's way where the wind's
    like a whetted² knife;
And all I ask is a merry yarn³ from a laughing fellow-rover,
And quiet sleep and a sweet dream when the long trick's⁴
    over.

---

¹**spume**   foam
²**whetted**   sharpened
³**yarn**   story
⁴**trick**   a turn steering the ship

Thoughts Like an Ocean

by Gareth Owen

The sea comes to me on the shore
On lacy slippered feet
And shyly, slyly slides away
With a murmur of defeat.

And as I stand there wondering
Strange thoughts spin round my head
Of why and where and what and when
And if not, why, what then?

Where do lobsters come from?
And where anemones?[1]
And are there other worlds out there
With other mysteries?

Why do *I* walk upon dry land
While fishes haunt the sea?
And as I think about their lives
Do they too think of me?

Why is water, water?
Why does it wet my hand?
Are there really as many stars
As there are grains of sand?

And where would the ocean go to
If there were no gravity?
And where was I before I lived?
And where's eternity?

---

[1]**anemones**   sea creatures

Perhaps the beach I'm standing on
Perhaps this stretch of sand
Perhaps the Universe itself
Lies on someone else's hand?

And isn't it strange how this water and I
At this moment happened to meet
And how this tide sweeps half the world
Before stopping at my feet.

Evidence

by Eiléan Ní Chuilleanáin

Along the wandering strand the sea unloads glass balls
Jellyfish, broken shells, its tangle
Of nets, cork, bits of wood,
Coral. A crooked line paid out on sand.
Here's evidence; gather it all up.

Time on window-panes
Imposes a curved edge of dust,
Hides dirt under the refrigerator, invites
The mice inside to dodge
Behind the revealing stack of empty bottles.
In the refrigerator the ice is growing
Into odd shapes; outside
The house, the cracks are spreading
In the asphalt;[1] they reach out, join
To weave some kind of message.

Age creates
People whose wrinkles betray
How they smiled, with scars
Of operations. They have white patches
Where the sun has not reached them:
The skin grows hard on their hands;
Some of them have false teeth.
The flick of their lashes, the flutter of their shirtfronts
Is evidence of life.

---

[1]**asphalt**   road surface

Tree Stump

by Moya Cannon

Thrown up
on the stones
in a bad November,

tree stump
returned from an exile
amongst fish and cormorants.[1]

For a week or a year
the ocean has salted your huge wound,
rocks have battered off your bark,
but the shipworms haven't riddled you.

Alive or dead,
there is little left of the slow strength
that filled a sky
when summer followed winter
and wind threw down the seeds.

I drag off bladderwrack[2]
to look at the years
and find, hugged hard in the wilderness of your roots,
lumps of granite
that stunted
and informed your growth.

---

[1]cormorants   sea birds
[2]bladderwrack   kind of seaweed

The Cherry Trees

by Laurence Binyon

Out of the dusk of distant woods
All round beneath the April skies
Blossom-white, the cherry trees
Like lovely apparitions[1] rise,

Like spirits strange to this ill world,
White strangers from a world apart,
Like silent promises of peace,
Like hope that blossoms in the heart.

---

[1]**apparitions**   visions

Loveliest of Trees, the Cherry Now

by A. E. Housman

Loveliest of trees, the cherry now
Is hung with bloom along the bough,
And stands about the woodland ride
Wearing white for Eastertide.

Now, of my threescore[1] years and ten,
Twenty will not come again,
And take from seventy springs a score,
It only leaves me fifty more.

And since to look at things in bloom
Fifty springs are little room,
About the woodlands I will go
To see the cherry hung with snow.

---

[1]**threescore**   three times a score (twenty), i.e. sixty

Stopping by Woods on a Snowy Evening
by Robert Frost

Whose woods these are I think I know.
His house is in the village though;
He will not see me stopping here
To watch his woods fill up with snow.

My little horse must think it queer
To stop without a farmhouse near
Between the woods and frozen lake
The darkest evening of the year.

He gives his harness bells a shake
To ask if there is some mistake.
The only other sound's the sweep
Of easy wind and downy flake.

The woods are lovely, dark and deep,
But I have promises to keep,
And miles to go before I sleep,
And miles to go before I sleep.

The Way Through the Woods
by Rudyard Kipling

They shut the road through the woods
Seventy years ago.
Weather and rain have undone it again,
And now you would never know
There was once a road through the woods
Before they planted the trees.
It is underneath the coppice[1] and heath,
And the thin anemones.[2]
Only the keeper sees
That, where the ring-dove broods,
And the badgers roll at ease,
There was once a road through the woods.

Yet, if you enter the woods
Of a summer evening late,
When the night-air cools on the trout-ringed pools
Where the otter whistles his mate,
(They fear not men in the woods,
Because they see so few.)
You will hear the beat of a horse's feet,
And the swish of a skirt in the dew,
Steadily cantering through
The misty solitudes,[3]
As though they perfectly knew
The old lost road through the woods . . .
But there is no road through the woods.

---

[1]**coppice**   grove of trees kept short by pruning
[2]**anemones**   white spring flowers
[3]**solitudes**   lonely places

In Time of 'The Breaking of Nations'
by Thomas Hardy

Only a man harrowing clods[1]
    In a slow silent walk
With an old horse that stumbles and nods
    Half asleep as they stalk.

Only thin smoke without flame
    From the heaps of couch-grass;
Yet this will go onward the same
    Though Dynasties[2] pass.

Yonder[3] a maid and her wight[4]
    Come whispering by:
War's annals[5] will cloud into night
    Ere their story die.

---

[1]**harrowing clods**   breaking up earth with harrows (similar to a plough)
[2]**Dynasties**   periods of rule
[3]**yonder**   over there
[4]**wight**   man
[5]**annals**   records

Uffington

by John Betjeman

Tonight we feel the muffled peal
    Hang on the village like a pall;[1]
It overwhelms the towering elms –
    That death-reminding dying fall;[2]
The very sky no longer high
    Comes down within the reach of all.
Imprisoned in a cage of sound
Even the trivial seems profound.

---

[1]**pall**   funeral shroud
[2]**dying fall**   fading note

Dumbshow

by John Montague

You'll have to run down to the shop:
my head dips, a dumbshow of assent,
as my aunt pens out the lengthening list
of articles no longer found on our musty shelf.

Windswift as Wilson, the *Wizard's* sprinting star,
I whip down the always widening Broad Road,
then huddle, hang around, hesitate in the dark
cavern at the back of Kelly's newer shop.

Until there is no one left, and then I try
to fishgasp something, but in the end
just push forward the scribbled grocery list
and nod eagerly, as each item is cleared off.

A gas lamp hangs its hissing circle
over the flitches[1] of lean and back bacon,
ropes of sausages, thick-crusted bread;
and all those words thronged in my head.

Every time I stand forth, fluent-tongued
in some foreign place, before an audience,
I am haunted, dogged by that mute lad,
as, warmly introduced, I step from the darkness.

---

[1]**flitches**   sides, cuts

Lucy Gray (or, Solitude)

by William Wordsworth

Oft I had heard of Lucy Gray:
And, when I crossed the wild,
I chanced to see at break of day
The solitary child.

No mate, no comrade Lucy knew;
She dwelt on a wide moor,
– The sweetest thing that ever grew
Beside a human door!

You yet may spy the fawn at play,
The hare upon the green;
But the sweet face of Lucy Gray
Will never more be seen.

'To-night will be a stormy night –
You to the town must go;
And take a lantern, Child, to light
Your mother through the snow.'

'That, Father! will I gladly do:
'Tis scarcely afternoon –
The minster-clock[1] has just struck two,
And yonder is the moon!'

At this the Father raised his hook,
And snapped a faggot-band;[2]
He plied his work; – and Lucy took
The lantern in her hand.

---

[1] **minster-clock**   clock of the parish church
[2] **faggot-band**   bunch of firewood

Not blither³ is the mountain roe:⁴
With many a wanton⁵ stroke
Her feet disperse the powdery snow,
That rises up like smoke.

The storm came on before its time:
She wandered up and down;
And many a hill did Lucy climb:
But never reached the town.

The wretched parents all that night
Went shouting far and wide;
But there was neither sound nor sight
To serve them for a guide.

At day-break on a hill they stood
That overlooked the moor;
And thence they saw the bridge of wood,
A furlong⁶ from their door.

They wept – and, turning homeward, cried,
'In Heaven we all shall meet;'
– When in the snow the mother spied
The print of Lucy's feet.

Then downwards from the steep hill's edge
They tracked the footmarks small;
And through the broken hawthorn hedge,
And by the long stone-wall;

---

³**blither**   happier
⁴**roe**   deer
⁵**wanton**   carefree
⁶**furlong**   eighth of a mile

And then an open field they crossed:
The marks were still the same;
They tracked them on, nor ever lost;
And to the bridge they came.

They followed from the snowy bank
Those footmarks, one by one,
Into the middle of the plank;
And further there were none!

– Yet some maintain that to this day
She is a living child;
That you may see sweet Lucy Gray
Upon the lonesome wild.

O'er rough and smooth she trips along,
And never looks behind;
And sings a solitary song
That whistles in the wind.

In the Attic

by Andrew Motion

Even though we know now
your clothes will never
be needed, we keep them,
upstairs in a locked trunk.

Sometimes I kneel there
touching them, trying to relive
time you wore them, to catch
the actual shape of arm and wrist.

My hands push down
between hollow, invisible sleeves,
hesitate, then take hold
and lift:

a green holiday; a red christening;
all your unfinished lives
fading through dark summers
entering my head as dust.

Drummer Hodge

by Thomas Hardy

They throw in Drummer Hodge, to rest
   Uncoffined – just as found:
His landmark is a kopje-crest[1]
   That breaks the veldt[2] around;
And foreign constellations west
   Each night above his mound.

Young Hodge the Drummer never knew –
   Fresh from his Wessex home –
The meaning of the broad Karoo,[3]
   The Bush, the dusty loam,[4]
And why uprose to nightly view
   Strange stars amid the gloam.[5]

Yet portion of that unknown plain
   Will Hodge for ever be;
His homely[6] Northern breast and brain
   Grow to some Southern tree,
And strange-eyed constellations reign
   His stars eternally.

---

[1]**kopje-crest**   top of a small, isolated hill
[2]**veldt**   open grassland
[3]**Karoo**   dry, flat area of South Africa
[4]**loam**   earth
[5]**gloam**   twilight
[6]**homely**   plain, unremarkable

High Flight (An Airman's Ecstasy)
by John Gillespie Magee

Oh! I have slipped the surly bonds of Earth
And danced the skies on laughter-silvered wings;
Sunward I've climbed and joined the tumbling mirth
Of sun-split clouds – and done a hundred things
You have not dreamed of – wheeled and soared and swung
High in the sunlit silence. Hovering there,
I've chased the shouting wind along, and flung
My eager craft through footless halls of air;
Up, up the long, delirious, burning blue
I've topped the wind-swept heights with easy grace,
Where never lark or even eagle flew;
And, while with silent lifting mind I've trod
The high untrespassed sanctity[1] of space,
Put out my hand and touched the face of God.

---

[1]**sanctity**   holiness

2000 AD

by Rabindranath Tagore

Who are you, reader, reading my poems an
hundred years hence?

I cannot send you one single flower
from this wealth of the spring, one single streak of gold
from yonder[1] clouds.

Open your doors and look abroad.

From your blossoming garden gather fragrant
memories of the vanished flowers of an hundred
years before.

In the joy of your heart may you feel
the living joy that sang one spring morning,
sending its glad voice across an hundred years.

---

[1] **yonder**   those over there

Activities

The Sea

1 The whole of this poem is an extended metaphor, describing the sea as a dog. In a small group, discuss how well you think the metaphor of the dog fits the sea. Try to think of other animals that would work. For example, could you write an effective poem beginning 'The sea is a thirsty cat . . . '?

Sea Fever

1 In a small group, read the poem aloud, preferably standing up. Notice the rhythm and the use of alliteration (e.g. the repeated 'w' sound in 'whale's way where the wind's like a whetted knife'). Discuss how the sound of the poem suggests the action of the sea.

2 Individually, pick out the details of the poem that you like best, and that most effectively make you think of the sea. What other details could the poet have used? Write an extra verse using them.

Thoughts Like an Ocean

1 The sea inspires this poet to think about the world. He begins with sea life and gradually builds up to thoughts on the universe as a whole. In a small group, brainstorm other questions like these that the sea might make you ask. Then divide them up into those that could be answered and those that are unanswerable. Why do you think the sea is such an inspiring force?

Evidence

1 a Each verse deals with a different type of 'evidence'. What are they? Working with a partner, jot down your answers.

 b Discuss what 'evidence' a stranger would find in your house, or in your room, to tell them about the people or person who lived there. For example, what might the CDs and DVDs you own say about your age, what might how your bedroom is decorated, or the types of food in the fridge reveal about you and those you live with?

 c Write two paragraphs about this evidence as if you were that stranger.

2   Individually, consider what 'evidence' there is of your likes and dislikes, your past, or your lifestyle in your appearance today. Draw a picture of yourself and label it accordingly.

Tree Stump

1   In a small group, discuss how this poem explores the theme of time – things changing and things enduring despite change. Do you think this poem is most about change or about things resisting change? Find evidence in the poem to support your view. Does each member of the group agree?

The Cherry Trees

1   This short poem is full of similes that say what the cherry trees are like. Identify them and write two or three paragraphs that discuss:
   * why the poet uses these particular similes
   * what adjectives you could use to describe the cherry trees as the poet sees them
   * what the overall mood of the poem is.

Loveliest of Trees, the Cherry Now

1   How old is the narrator of this poem? Think of all the possible ways in which this might relate to the appearance of the cherry tree at the time of year described. Make a mind map or spider diagram to show your ideas.

Stopping by Woods on a Snowy Evening

1   Discuss these questions with a partner:
   * Does the simple language of this poem reflects its subject and the mood of the narrator?
   * What would be emphasised in a painting of this subject?
   * If you were standing next to the narrator with your eyes shut, what would you hear and feel?

Make notes so that you can share your ideas with another group or the rest of the class.

The Way Through the Woods

1   What animals are mentioned in this poem? How do they add to the mood of the poem? Discuss your thoughts with a partner.

2   There is an air of mystery about this poem, partly created by the repetition of the phrases 'the woods' and 'road through the woods'. It could be read as a ghost story – what events do you think could lie behind it? Tell your version of the story to your partner; you might like to write it down so you can share it with the rest of the class or another pair.

3   If the lost road in the woods is a symbol (something standing for something else), what do you think it could symbolise? With your partner, make notes or a mind map to record your ideas.

In Time of 'The Breaking of Nations'

1   Thomas Hardy wrote this poem in 1915 – during World War I, a time of huge change. The poem looks at the things that will carry on despite these changes. Do you agree with his choices? What might these choices represent? Record your thoughts using a mind map.

2   Create a two-column table. In one column, list things from your own daily life that you think will have changed radically or disappeared in a hundred years' time. In the other column, list things that will probably remain more or less the same.

Uffington

1   Discuss these questions with a partner:
   ● What is the mood of the poem? How is this achieved?
   ● The poem describes the ringing of church bells, a regular feature of Betjeman's poetry. What is their effect? (Notice especially the last two lines.)

Dumbshow

1 Discuss the following questions in a small group:

- How does the boy see himself in the second verse, and how is this impression helped by the alliteration of words beginning with 'w'?
- How does this contrast with how he behaves when he arrives at the shop?
- Why does he 'try to fishgasp something', and how does this contrast with what he is like as an adult in the final verse?
- Why is the poet 'haunted' by this memory of himself as a boy?

Lucy Gray (or, Solitude)

1 This simply told ballad is clearly a sad story but there is a mystery about what has actually happened to Lucy Gray (see the last three verses). What is the mystery, and what do you think has happened to her? Write a news story about her disappearance. Include:

- Lucy's age
- what errand she was sent on, and who by
- the weather
- her parents' efforts to find her.

In the Attic

1 a Discuss the following questions in a small group:

- Who do you think the poet is addressing in this poem?
- Why might the clothes be kept 'in a locked trunk' in the attic?
- Why does the poet put his hands into the clothes?

b Share your ideas with another group. Did you reach similar conclusions or were your ideas different?

Drummer Hodge

1 Thomas Hardy is writing about a young soldier (probably a teenager) who has died in the Boer War, in South Africa. Discuss the following questions with a partner:

- How does the style of the poem reflect the fact that Hodge was a simple country boy?

• What is described in the final verse, and what is strange or remarkable about this happening to a young man who had probably never been far from his village before being sent abroad?

2 Imagine Hodge is finally given a gravestone. Write a suitable epitaph to go on it. It could be in verse or prose.

High Flight (An Airman's Ecstasy)

1 a Read the poem aloud. Then discuss, in a small group, how its language, including alliteration (e.g. 'slipped . . . surly . . . skies'), reflects the poet's love of flying.

b This poem is a sonnet (it has fourteen lines and a structured rhyme scheme). Find out what you can about the sonnet. Why do you think John Gillespie Magee chose this form for his poem about flight?

2000 AD

1 The poet addresses this poem to an imagined reader a hundred years on. Taking ideas from his poem, write a poem of your own addressed to an imaginary reader a hundred years from now. Before you begin, decide how much you want to tell the reader about the time and place you are writing in (Rabindranath Tagore says very little about his life in 1900, but you may want to go into more detail). You could begin your poem with the same opening lines or make up your own.

Compare and contrast

1 a *The Sea* and *Sea Fever* are obviously both about the sea, but how similar are they? Working with a partner or in a small group, draw up two lists headed 'Similarities' and 'Differences'. When discussing them, try to answer the following questions:
- Which poem gives a more vivid idea of what the sea is like, and how?
- Which expresses the poet's feelings about the sea more vividly?
- What details does each describe?
- How do their narrators differ in character and attitude towards the sea?

   b Write one or two paragraphs comparing the two poems. Remember to add short quotations to back up your points. Finish by saying which poem gives you a more vivid idea of what the sea is like, and why.

2 Imagine that Laurence Binyon (*The Cherry Trees*) and A. E. Housman (*Loveliest of Trees, the Cherry Now*) have both submitted their poems to be included in the Spring issue of your poetry magazine. In a small group (ideally of five), consider which should be included. Nominate at least one person from your group to defend the Binyon and at least one person to defend the Housman poem. They should present their arguments to the final member of the group, who must make the final decision between the two poems.

   When making your case for either of the poems, consider the following questions:
- How does the poet use imagery? How effectively does he create a picture of the cherry tree?
- Does the poet tell us something about himself?
- What atmosphere, or feeling, is created in the poem?

3 a Working with a partner, compare the moods of *Stopping by Woods on a Snowy Evening* and *The Way Through the Woods*. You should each identify, then share and write down, particular words and phrases that help to create these moods. Think about:

- whether the moods created are similar or different
- which techniques or devices the poets have employed to help create the atmosphere.

b Still working with your partner, prepare a short talk for your class comparing the moods of these poems. End by saying which you prefer, and why. Your presentation may be more engaging if you and your partner take opposing viewpoints.

4 a *In Time of 'The Breaking of Nations'* and *Dumbshow* both consider the idea of change. In a table, record the phrases from each poem that seem to be about:

- things that are unlikely to change
- things that have changed.

b In what ways do the poems tackle the idea of change differently? Write a paragraph comparing the views of change given in these poems.

5 Imagine the ghosts of Drummer Hodge and the narrator of *High Flight* meet up and share their different experiences of war. Script their dialogue. Think about:

- how each man felt about his experience of war
- how each man's experience was different
- their different social backgrounds (notice the airman's choice of words).

Lay out your script with the speakers' names shown clearly: HODGE and AIRMAN.

5 Digging deeper

The poems in this section are particularly thought-provoking, and you should find yourself 'digging deeper' into their meaning, and into how the poets use words to express that meaning. Some of the poems explore uncertainty, and you may find yourself uncertain of their exact meaning. You may wonder why the heart of the man in *House on a Cliff* is locked; you may sense an urgent threat in *O What Is That Sound* but not be able to say what it is. If so, don't worry! Every reader must start from their personal idea of what the poem is about.

These poems raise as many questions as they answer, and you should find a lot to discuss, from what the man on the frozen railway station platform in *Missing the Troop Train* will do next to 'what immortal hand or eye' created William's Blake's Tyger.

Activities

1 a Some of the poems in this section create a strong atmosphere by the language they use. What ideas and feelings do the following atmospheric phrases suggest to you?
   - *A haze of thunder hangs on the hospital rose-beds* (Five O'Clock Shadow)
   - *Outdoors the chill, the void, the siren* (House on a Cliff)
   - *. . . the light of an electric lamp / Rocking in a small station at night* (Missing the Troop Train)
   - *Flies clung in clumps on their sweat-scented backs* (Stanley Meets Mutesa)
   - *. . . boundless and bare / The lone and level sands stretch far away* (Ozymandias)

   b Write a poem beginning with one of these phrases, trying to maintain the same atmosphere.

2 Working with a partner or individually, write the quotes below, which are taken from poems in this section, on a large sheet of paper. Add pictures to illustrate them. If you prefer, you could write 'illustration briefs': short instructions for an illustrator.

- *Indoors the locked heart and the lost key* (*House on a Cliff*)
- *Regiments, divisions, armies of stars* (*Missing the Troop Train*)
- *. . . the hollow wood / Where birds swim like fish* (*The Hollow Wood*)
- *When the stars threw down their spears* (*The Tyger*)

3 a Animals are often used to symbolise or explore different ideas. Some of the poems in this section use this device. Imagine that these animals can talk. Choose three of them. For each one write a sentence that it might say that would express its character.

- seagulls
- vultures
- goldfinches (small brightly coloured birds)
- dolphins
- donkeys.

b Think about why we associate certain animals with certain characteristics. Discuss in a small group other instances in which you have seen any of the animals in the list above, or that feature in the poems in this section, portrayed. This might be other poems, books, on television, in films or from real-life experience. Are these animals always portrayed in the same light?

4 a Some of the poems in this section are about people under the stress of uncertainty – not knowing what is going to happen. With a partner, discuss how this stress affects young people today.

b Either   Write a short story about a young person under stress.

Or   Write a magazine article about reducing stress.

There Are Days

by John Montague

There are days when
one should be able
to pluck off one's head
like a dented or worn
helmet, straight from
the nape[1] and collarbone
(those crackling branches!)

and place it firmly down
in the bed of a flowing stream.
Clear, clean, chill currents
coursing[2] and spuming[3] through
the sour and stale compartments
of the brain, dimmed eardrums,
bleared eyesockets, filmed tongue.

And then set it back again
on the base of the shoulders:
well tamped[4] down, of course,
the laved[5] skin and mouth,
the marble of the eyes
rinsed and ready
for love; for prophecy?[6]

---

[1]**nape**   back of neck
[2]**coursing**   racing
[3]**spuming**   foaming
[4]**tamped**   pushed
[5]**laved**   washed
[6]**prophecy**   prediction

Five O'Clock Shadow

by John Betjeman

This is the time of day when we in the Men's Ward
    Think 'One more surge of the pain and I give up the fight,'
When he who struggles for breath can struggle less strongly:
    This is the time of day which is worse than night.

A haze of thunder hangs on the hospital rose-beds,
    A doctors' foursome out on the links[1] is played,
Safe in her sitting-room Sister is putting her feet up:
    This is the time of day when we feel betrayed.

Below the windows, loads of loving relations
    Rev in the car park, changing gear at the bend,
Making for home and a nice big tea and the telly:
    'Well, we've done what we can. It can't be long till the end.'

This is the time of day when the weight of bedclothes
    Is harder to bear than a sharp incision of steel.
The endless anonymous croak of a cheap transistor[2]
    Intensifies the lonely terror I feel.

---

[1]**links**   golf course
[2]**transistor**   small radio

Guardians

by John Montague

In my sick daughter's room
the household animals gather.
Our black Tom poses lordly on
the sun-warmed windowsill.
A spaniel sleeps by her slippers,
keeping one weather eye open.
For once, they agree to differ:
nary[1] a sound, or spit of bother.
Aloof and hieratic[2] as guardians,
they seem wiser than this poor animal,
her father, tiptoeing in and out,
ferrying water-bottle, elixirs, fruit,
his unaccustomed stockinged stealth
tuned anxiously to a child's breath.

[1] **nary**   not
[2] **hieratic**   priestly

A Dream

by Dermot Healy

I had a dream
in which Jimmy Foley died
in the back room.

I lived out towards the front
oblivious[1] of his hunger
for days and days.

And when they said
'But he's in your house!'
I didn't believe them.

I started to explain
but my voice grew distant
and eerie.

My anxiety was choking me
that I could have been such a fool
to let Jimmy die in my own house.

Imagine my relief on wakening!
To see the light still burning
in his window.

And then I thought of my mother
who had forgotten to feed her sister,
with Maisie sitting diligently in her room

---

[1]**oblivious**   unaware

afraid to walk for fear of falling.
And when I pushed open the door and asked her,
'Have you not eaten yet?'

she said, 'It's alright. Someone will come.'
Her faith shy and absolute.
Then mother remembers.

Soon everyone is running to feed Maisie.
And maybe that is why I dreamed
Jimmy dead.

In the world of dream
where anxiety can never be appeased[2]
everyone has someone dying of hunger.

---

[2]**appeased**   calmed with a peace-offering

House on a Cliff

by Louis MacNeice

Indoors the tang[1] of a tiny oil lamp. Outdoors
The winking signal on the waste of sea.
Indoors the sound of the wind. Outdoors the wind.
Indoors the locked heart and the lost key.

Outdoors the chill, the void, the siren. Indoors
The strong man pained to find his red blood cools,
While the blind clock grows louder, faster. Outdoors
The silent moon, the garrulous[2] tides she rules.

Indoors ancestral curse-cum-blessing. Outdoors
The empty bowl of heaven, the empty deep.
Indoors a purposeful man who talks at cross
Purposes, to himself, in a broken sleep.

---

[1]**tang**   sharp smell
[2]**garrulous**   talkative

In a Non-Sleeper

by Boris Slutsky (translated by Elaine Feinstein)

In a non-sleeper, without reserved places,
one passenger sleeps restlessly, as if
in a city under occupation, his
bundle kept under his side continuously.

Yet theft is a thing of the past, surely
all robbers have been locked away.
Just go to sleep, and if you don't fall off
your seat, there's time to scan your dreams enjoyably.

But he lies awkwardly drawn up
                      and cramped
his fingers clenched into a fist;
he sleeps as if his bundle must
contain important secret information.

In here there's light and heating, even
an unreserved carriage isn't so bad:
but things that happened once in
other times than these persist, and
cast their shadows on his lips.

Yes, the man sleeps as if still in the war:
uneasily
           as though afraid to make
some terrible mistake
               while he is sleeping.

Missing the Troop Train

by Yevgeny Vinokurov
(translated by Daniel Weissbort)

There's something desperate about trains . . .
I stood alone on the icy platform,
Lost in the Bashkir steppes.[1]
What can be more fantastic, more desolate
Than the light of an electric lamp
Rocking in a small station at night?
Trains swept past from time to time.
Their roar engulfed me,
I was submerged in coal dust,
And each time, I grabbed hold of my cap –
It looked as though I was greeting someone.
The bare, stunted tree by the side of the platform
Reached out after them . . .
I waited for one train at least
to stop, for god's sake!
In the distance was the dark forest mass.
I lifted my head –
over me, a vast
Host of stars:
Regiments,
             divisions,
                       armies of stars,
All bound for somewhere.

---

[1] **steppes**   wide, grassy, treeless plains

An hour earlier, I'd got out of the train
To fetch some boiling water . . .
I could be court-martialled for this.
I stood there,
the snow melted round my boots,
And the water in the aluminium kettle I was holding
Had already iced over.
Above the forest mass, I saw
A little star,
Fallen a long way behind the others.
I looked at it
And it looked at me.

O What Is That Sound

by W. H. Auden

O what is that sound which so thrills the ear
   Down in the valley drumming, drumming?
Only the scarlet soldiers, dear,
   The soldiers coming.

O what is that light I see flashing so clear
   Over the distance brightly, brightly?
Only the sun on their weapons, dear,
   As they step lightly.

O what are they doing with all that gear,
   What are they doing this morning, this morning?
Only their usual manoeuvres,[1] dear,
   Or perhaps a warning.

O why have they left the road down there,
   Why are they suddenly wheeling,[2] wheeling?
Perhaps a change in their orders, dear.
   Why are you kneeling?

O haven't they stopped for the doctor's care,
   Haven't they reined their horses, their horses?
Why, they are none of them wounded, dear,
   None of these forces.

O is it the parson they want, with white hair,
   Is it the parson, is it, is it?
No, they are passing his gateway, dear,
   Without a visit.

---

[1]**manoeuvres**   army practice
[2]**wheeling**   turning, changing direction

O it must be the farmer who lives so near.
　It must be the farmer so cunning, so cunning?
They have passed the farmyard already, dear,
　And now they are running.

O where are you going? Stay with me here!
　Were the vows you swore deceiving, deceiving?
No, I promised to love you, dear,
　But I must be leaving.

O it's broken the lock and splintered the door,
　O it's the gate where they're turning, turning;
Their boots are heavy on the floor
　And their eyes are burning.

Stanley Meets Mutesa[1]

by David Rubadiri

Such a time of it they had;
The heat of the day
The chill of the night
And the mosquitoes that followed.
Such was the time and
They bound for a kingdom.

The thin weary line of carriers
With tattered dirty rags to cover their backs;
The battered bulky chests
That kept on falling off their shaven heads.
Their tempers high and hot
The sun fierce and scorching
With it rose their spirits
With its fall their hopes
As each day sweated their bodies dry and
Flies clung in clumps on their sweat-scented backs.
Such was the march
And the hot season just breaking.

Each day a weary pony dropped,
Left for the vultures on the plains;
Each afternoon a human skeleton collapsed,
Left for the Masai[2] on the plains;
But the march trudged on
Its Khaki leader in front
He the spirit that inspired.
He the light of hope.

---

[1]**Stanley . . . Mutesa**   the explorer Henry Stanley and King Mutesa of
   Buganda
[2]**Masai**   African tribe

Then came the afternoon of a hungry march,
A hot and hungry march it was;
The Nile and the Nyanza[3]
Lay like two twins
Azure across the green countryside.
The march leapt on chaunting
Like young gazelles to a water hole.
Hearts beat faster
Loads felt lighter
As the cool water lapt their sore soft feet.
No more the dread of hungry hyenas
But only tales of valour when
At Mutesa's court fires are lit.
No more the burning heat of the day
But song, laughter and dance.
The village looks on behind banana groves,
Children peer behind reed fences.
Such was the welcome
No singing women to chaunt a welcome
Or drums to greet the white ambassador;
Only a few silent nods from aged faces
And one rumbling drum roll
To summon Mutesa's court to parley[4]
For the country was not sure.

---

[3]**Nile . . . Nyanza**   rivers
[4]**parley**   talk, as in peace talks

The gate of reeds is flung open,
There is silence
But only a moment's silence –
A silence of assessment.
The tall black king steps forward,
He towers over the thin bearded white man
Then grabbing his lean white hand
Manages to whisper
'Mtu Mweupe karibu'
White man you are welcome.
The gate of polished reed closes behind them
And the west is let in.

Ozymandias

by Percy Bysshe Shelley

I met a traveller from an antique land
Who said: Two vast and trunkless[1] legs of stone
Stand in the desert . . . Near them, on the sand,
Half sunk, a shattered visage[2] lies, whose frown,
And wrinkled lip, and sneer of cold command,
Tell that its sculptor well those passions read
Which yet survive, stamped on these lifeless things,
The hand that mocked[3] them, and the heart that fed:
And on the pedestal these words appear:
'My name is Ozymandias, king of kings:
Look on my works, ye Mighty, and despair!'
Nothing beside remains. Round the decay
Of that colossal wreck, boundless and bare
The lone and level sands stretch far away.

---

[1]**trunkless**   without upper body
[2]**visage**   face
[3]**mocked**   copied

Call to a Simple Feast

by Sue Minish

In this blue dish, a world:
Pale avocado slices
Ripened on a scorched kibbutz,[1]
Shredded carrot from the Lutheran[2] low-lands
Mix with apple-dice picked in orchards
Where it is already tomorrow,
And damp raisins soak up the royal blood
Of beets harvested by solemn Poles,
As they have for a thousand years.

The hot-headed scallions[3]
And soft-hearted greens,
Gifts from a small farm,
Shine with the oil of Spanish olives
And sharp French cider spiked
With garlic, peppers and coarse crystals
From shining salt pans[4] far to the south,
Crushed and ground together.
Harmony, in this blue dish at least.

---

[1]**kibbutz**   communal farm in Israel
[2]**Lutheran**   from a place in Germany
[3]**scallions**   young onions
[4]**salt pans**   place where water evaporates, leaving salt

Charms

by Catherine Phil MacCarthy

Thistles. Nettles.
In the long grass,
a hot afternoon.

The calves of my legs
stung. Dock leaves
rubbed to juice

trickled green
on the burn.
What time was it then?

I reached for
dandelion clocks.
Whispered your name.

Whole moons frayed
under my breath.
One o'clock, two,

loves me, loves me
not. The answer?
A bald stem.

The Hollow Wood

by Edward Thomas

Out in the sun the goldfinch flits
Along the thistle-tops, flits and twits
Above the hollow wood
Where birds swim like fish –
Fish that laugh and shriek –
To and fro, far below
In the pale hollow wood.

Lichen, ivy, and moss
Keep evergreen the trees
That stand half-flayed and dying,
And the dead trees on their knees
In dog's-mercury[1] and moss:
And the bright twit of the goldfinch drops
Down there as he flits on thistle-tops.

---

[1]**dog's-mercury**   a woodland plant

Watching for Dolphins
by David Constantine

In the summer months on every crossing to Piraeus[1]
One noticed that certain passengers soon rose
From seats in the packed saloon and with serious
Looks and no acknowledgement of a common purpose
Passed forward through the small door into the bows
To watch for dolphins. One saw them lose

Every other wish. Even the lovers
Turned their desires on the sea, and a fat man
Hung with equipment to photograph the occasion
Stared like a saint, through sad bi-focals; others,
Hopeless themselves, looked to the children for they
Would see dolphins if anyone would. Day after day

Or on their last opportunity all gazed
Undecided whether a flat calm were favourable
Or a sea the sun and the wind between them raised
To a likeness of dolphins. Were gulls a sign, that fell
Screeching from the sky or over an unremarkable place
Sat in a silent school? Every face

After its character implored[2] the sea.
All, unaccustomed, wanted epiphany,[3]
Praying the sky would clang and the abused Aegean[4]
Reverberate[5] with cymbal, gong and drum.
We could not imagine more prayer, and had they then
On the waves, on the climax of our longing come

---

[1]**Piraeus**   a Greek city
[2]**implored**   begged
[3]**epiphany**   sudden appearance of divine being, sudden understanding
[4]**Aegean**   part of the Mediterranean Sea
[5]**reverberate**   vibrate with noise

Smiling, snub-nosed, domed like satyrs,[6] oh
We should have laughed and lifted the children up
Stranger to stranger, pointing how with a leap
They left their element, three or four times, centred
On grace, and heavily and warm re-entered,
Looping the keel. We should have felt them go

Further and further into the deep parts. But soon
We were among the great tankers, under their chains
In black water. We had not seen the dolphins
But woke, blinking. Eyes cast down
With no admission of disappointment the company
Dispersed and prepared to land in the city.

---

[6]**satyrs**   mythical goat-like creatures

The Donkey

by G. K. Chesterton

When fishes flew and forests walked
    And figs grew upon thorn,
Some moment when the moon was blood
    Then surely I was born.

With monstrous head and sickening cry
    And ears like errant[1] wings,
The devil's walking parody[2]
    On all four-footed things.

The tattered outlaw of the earth,
    Of ancient crooked will;
Starve, scourge,[3] deride me: I am dumb,
    I keep my secret still.

Fools! For I also had my hour;
    One far fierce hour and sweet:
There was a shout about my ears,
    And palms before my feet.

[1]**errant**   straying
[2]**parody**   joke version
[3]**scourge**   whip

The Tyger

by William Blake

Tyger! Tyger! burning bright
In the forests of the night,
What immortal hand or eye
Could frame thy fearful symmetry?

In what distant deeps or skies
Burnt the fire of thine eyes?
On what wings dare he aspire?[1]
What the hand dare seize the fire?

And what shoulder, and what art,
Could twist the sinews of thy heart?
And, when thy heart began to beat,
What dread hand? and what dread feet?

What the hammer? what the chain?
In what furnace was thy brain?
What the anvil?[2] what dread grasp
Dare its deadly terrors clasp?

When the stars threw down their spears,
And water'd heaven with their tears,
Did he smile his work to see?
Did he who made the Lamb make thee?

Tyger! Tyger! burning bright
In the forests of the night,
What immortal hand or eye,
Dare frame thy fearful symmetry?

---

[1] **aspire**   hope
[2] **anvil**   iron form on which blacksmith hammers metal

Activities

There Are Days

1 Imagine that the course of action described in this poem were actually possible. Write a set of instructions for someone wishing to try it. At the end, list some of the possible benefits they should experience.

2 Write a short story about someone who follows the procedure described in the poem. Use these questions to help you plan the story:
- Why do they need to do it?
- Do they behave differently after doing it?
- What happens to them as a result?

Five O'Clock Shadow

1 In a small group, discuss the situation of the narrator of this poem and what he finds so awful about this time of day.

2 Write your own poem beginning 'This is the time of day' about a time of day that you particularly like or dislike. Try to include at least three verses. Perhaps you enjoy the quiet of the early morning, or dislike the time just before you go to bed each evening. Make your poem as detailed as possible.

Guardians

1 This is a very visual poem. Read it at least once and then discuss with a partner the picture it creates. Does it remind you of any particular style of painting?

2 Write a letter from the father/narrator to a relative about his sick daughter and how he is looking after her. Be sure to express his concern for her. Mention the animals too: you could give the spaniel a name.

A Dream

1 In a small group, discuss how the conversational style of this poem makes the dream seem more realistic.

2 Re-read the final verse. How much truth do you think there is in the idea that in dreams anxiety can never be 'appeased' and 'everyone has someone dying of hunger'? Share your thoughts with the rest of the class.

House on a Cliff

1 Read the poem aloud with a partner, with one person reading all the 'Indoors' lines and the other all the 'Outdoors' lines. Then read it aloud again, this time with one person reading all the 'Indoors' lines one after the other, and the other person reading all the 'Outdoors' lines one after the other. How is this second version of the poem different? Does this version make it easier to focus on the character of the man indoors?

2 With a partner, or on your own, write your own Indoors–Outdoors poem. Choose from one of these examples or use your own idea.
- A child inside a car travelling on the motorway
- An old woman outside a warm and busy hotel or public house
- A teenager inside a quiet classroom in an inner-city school.

In a Non-Sleeper

1 In a small group, discuss the following questions:
- What country is the poem set in? Look in particular at the line 'Yet theft is a thing of the past, surely' (the poet is saying that the government claims this to be true).
- What do you think could be in the man's 'bundle'?
- What kind of things do you think happened 'once in / other times'?
- Why do you suppose the man seems afraid, even in his sleep?

Missing the Troop Train

1 This poem tells a story about how the narrator came to be standing on a freezing station platform at night, in the middle of the

Russian steppes. Make notes using a spider diagram to gather facts from the poem. Use your notes to continue his story by adding a new verse to the poem.

O What Is That Sound

1 The poem is in the form of a conversation between a man and his wife or lover. With a partner, discuss what the male character is trying to do in this conversation and how the details describing the soldiers create a growing tension that works against his efforts.

2 There seems to be a story behind this poem. With a partner, work out what you think the story is. Then, individually, write an account of what events may have led to the scene described in the poem. What might happen next?

Stanley Meets Mutesa

1 This poem tells how the explorer Henry Stanley met King Mutesa of Buganda in 1875, after a long journey across Africa. In a small group, discuss what details most vividly reveal what a difficult time Stanley and his team had, and what details show how things eventually improved.

2 Write three diary entries for Stanley, the first two on his journey, and the third after he has just met the King.

Ozymandias

1 What sort of man do you think Ozymandias was? How can you tell from the poem? Write an account of him having the statue of himself made. Use the line that Shelley quotes and try to make the Egyptian's character come across in your account.

2 The line supposedly spoken by Ozymandias has an ironic double meaning. He intended other leaders to despair of ever being as great as him. Why else might they despair now, on seeing the ruins of his statue? With this in mind, write two or three paragraphs explaining what point Shelley is making in this poem.

Call to a Simple Feast

1 This poem gives us a picture of a world of foods combining in harmony. What might the blue dish itself represent? Compare your answer with a partner's.

2 List the ingredients in the poem and write a set of instructions, in the style of a cookery book, for preparing this dish.

Charms

1 Discuss the following questions in a small group:
   • Why do you think the poem is called 'Charms'?
   • What is the mood of the poem?
   • Who do you think the poem is addressed to ('Whispered your name')?
   • What does the poet seem to be saying about folk remedies and customs?

The Hollow Wood

1 The poem contrasts a sunlit hillside with the wood below. With a partner, discuss how the two places are different. List the words and phrases associated with each, and what they suggest to you.

Watching for Dolphins

1 In a small group, discuss the passengers' thoughts about the dolphins. Then use your ideas in an improvisation of the boat trip to Piraeus in which you speak their thoughts out loud. Divide it into three scenes:
   • The passengers are hoping to see dolphins. Try to express a sense of 'longing'.
   • Pretend that the dolphins have finally appeared. (See the second-to-last verse.)
   • Return to reality: the dolphins did not appear during this trip. Instead of making 'no admission of disappointment', the passengers share their feelings about this.

The Donkey

1 Do you agree with the judgement on donkeys expressed in verse 2? Write an alternative verse showing the donkey in a better light.

2 The final verse refers to Jesus entering Jerusalem riding a donkey on Palm Sunday. If possible, read the Bible's account in Matthew 21: 1–11. Then write your own version from the viewpoint of the donkey or a bystander.

The Tyger

1 In a small group, read the poem aloud. Notice its powerful rhythm. Rehearse a reading in which the whole group reads the first and last verses and individuals take it in turns to read one question in the verses in between.

2 There are a lot of questions in this poem. But behind them, Blake is really asking one big question about life. In a small group, discuss what this question is.

Compare and contrast

1 a   Make notes on the different ways in which illness is presented in *Five O'Clock Shadow* and *Guardians*. Include the details and phrases that you think are especially important.

 b   Write medical reports on each of the patients in the poems saying how they are and what their prospects are.

2   *House on a Cliff* and *The Hollow Wood* both present contrasts. Compare the ways in which they do this using a table like the one below:

	House on a Cliff	The Hollow Wood
Detail to describe places		
Similes and metaphors		
What each is really about, in your view		
The 'voice' of the poet		

3   *In a Non-Sleeper* and *Missing the Troop Train* are both by Russian poets. Write answers in sentences to the following questions.

 a   What views of train travel does each give?

 b   What does each say about authority?

 c   What information does each give about war?

 d   What can you find that might be especially Russian about them?

4   Write about the different presentations of foreign lands, customs and travel offered in *Stanley Meets Mutesa* and *Ozymandias*. In your answer, consider:

 ●   how each poem uses setting to create atmosphere

 ●   how the two kings Mutesa and Ozymandias are similar or dissimilar

 ●   how each poem, in its own way, is about things changing with time.

5 a   It could be said that *Charms*, *Watching for Dolphins* and *O What Is That Sound* are all about expectations (or hopes) and disappointment. For each poem, make a list or mind map of what these expectations and disappointments are.

b   Write a paragraph or two explaining which poem you think gives the strongest feeling of disappointment, and how it achieves that.

6   *The Donkey* and *The Tyger* both use individual animals to explore different ideas. Compare them using a table like the one below:

	The Donkey	*The Tyger*
Who 'speaks' the poem?		
How is the animal portrayed?		
What does the poem say about the animal's creation?		
What hidden message could there be in the poem?		

Notes on authors

Simon Armitage (1963–) lives in Huddersfield and is a very well-known British poet. He is also a playwright, travel writer and song lyricist. For more information on Simon Armitage and his writing visit http://www.simonarmitage.com.

W. H. Auden (1907–73) was born in York, but grew up in Birmingham before moving to the USA in 1939. He is perhaps most well known for his poetry, particularly *Funeral Blues* which was featured in the 1990s' hit film *Four Weddings and a Funeral*. He was also a playwright and novelist.

James Berry (1924–) is a Jamaican-born writer who has a particular interest in multi-cultural education and Black British writing. In 1990 he was awarded the OBE for services to poetry. He now lives in Brighton and divides his time between the UK and Jamaica.

John Betjeman (1906–84) was a poet, writer and broadcaster with a keen interest in architecture. In the 1950s and 60s he led various campaigns to save threatened buildings and presented several television documentaries. In 1969 he was knighted and he became Poet Laureate in 1972.

Laurence Binyon (1869–1943) was an English poet, playwright and art scholar. He is perhaps best known for his World War I poetry – *For the Fallen* is often used in Remembrance Sunday services.

Sheila Glen Bishop lives in Somerset. Her works include a book for children, *Joe and the Caterpillar* (William Heinemann Ltd, 1972) and a volume of poetry, *Snailshells or Butterflies* (National Poetry Foundation, 1992).

William Blake (1757–1827) was born in London. He never went to school, instead attending drawing classes and becoming apprentice to an engraver at 14. A poet, painter and printmaker, he was largely unrecognised in his own lifetime.

Rupert Brooke (1887–1915) is known for producing war poetry that reflected the initial idealism felt about World War I. He survived the disastrous Antwerp expedition of 1914 with the Royal Naval Division, but died at the age of just 27 in 1915, after a simple mosquito bite turned septic.

Colette Bryce (1970–) won the National Poetry Competition in 2003. She was born in Northern Ireland and has produced several collections of poetry, including *Self-Portrait in the Dark* (Picador, 2008). She currently lives in London.

Abena P. A. Busia (1953–) was born in Ghana, where her father was a politician until the whole family was forced into exile in England. She currently works as a Professor of English in America and is co-director of the Women Writing Africa Project. She writes short stories and poetry as well as non-fiction.

Joseph Campbell (1879–1944) was born in Belfast. He lived briefly in both London and the USA but always returned to Ireland and remained involved in Irish literary activities. He founded the Ulster Literary Theatre in 1905.

Moya Cannon (1956–) is an Irish poet. She was editor of *Poetry Ireland Review* in 1995 and has been a writer-in-residence at Trent University, Ontario, and at the Centre Culturel Irlandais, Paris. She is perhaps best known for her award-winning collection of poems entitled *Oar* (Salmon Publishing, 1992).

Charles Causley (1917–2003) was born in Launcaston, Cornwall and lived there throughout his life. His father died in World War I and he himself served in World War II. He was inspired by folk songs, hymns and ballads and in 1967 was awarded the Queen's Gold Medal for poetry.

Prem Chaya (1915–81) is primarily known as a translator and poet. One of Thailand's most prominent literary figures, his full name was Prince Prem Purachatra.

G. K. Chesterton (1874-1936) was a prolific and diverse writer, producing poetry, philosophy, journalism, biography, novels and political works.

Eiléan Ní Chuilleanáin (1942-) is an Irish poet who has produced several collections of poetry. Some of her most distinctive works can be found in *Selected Poems* (Faber and Faber, 2008). She is married to fellow Irish poet Macdara Woods.

Colley Cibber (1671-1757) worked in London as a playwright and actor, as well as writing poetry. In 1730 he was made Poet Laureate, although his work was not admired by his contemporaries; many believed that the honour was in fact a reward for his unwavering support of Robert Walpole, the prime minister.

John Clare (1793-1864) was born in Northamptonshire and is now considered to be one of the most important poets of the 19th century. He received very little formal education and was constantly torn between the literary world of London and his illiterate roots. He suffered from general poor health and alcoholism, and died in an asylum.

Gillian Clarke (1937-) is a Welsh poet who has featured heavily in the GSCE and A level English examinations for many years. She currently lives in Ceredigion, Wales, where she runs an organic small-holding and continues to write. More information about Gillian Clarke can be found at http://www.gillianclarke.co.uk.

Pádraic Colum (1881-1972) was born in County Longford, Ireland. He worked as a poet, novelist, biographer and dramatist, and was co-founder of the literary journal *The Irish Review*. He emigrated to the USA in 1914 and remained there until his death.

David Constantine (1944-) was born in Salford, Lancashire. He is currently a fellow at Queen's College, Oxford as well as working as a poet, author and translator.

Robert Frost (1874-1963) was an American poet whose realistic depictions of rural life gained him four Pulitzer prizes for poetry. His working life was spent as an English teacher and included a brief spell in Britain (1912-1915).

Douglas Gibson was an English novelist, poet and war correspondent.

Philip Gross (1952–) began writing at a young age and has published a wide range of works, including poetry, short stories and opera libretti. He currently lives in Bristol and is Professor of Creative Writing for the University of Glamorgan.

Thomas Hardy (1840–1928) was born and spent most of his life in Dorset. After an unsuccessful first attempt at poetry he enjoyed fame and critical success through his novels, which were often set in the Dorset countryside. He returned to writing poetry and enjoyed success from work produced in his 70s.

Dermot Healy (1947–) is an Irish novelist, playwright and poet. He currently lives in County Sligo in Ireland.

Seamus Heaney (1939–) is an Irish-born poet. He began writing when he got his first teaching appointment in Belfast. He continues to live in Ireland, but spends some time in America teaching. In 1995 he won the Nobel Prize for Literature.

John Hegley (1953–) is a performance poet and songwriter. He performs on the radio, on television, in the theatre and at festivals. Much of his work is aimed at younger audiences.

Phoebe Hesketh (1909–2005) was born in Preston, Lancashire. She produced sixteen books and also worked as a freelance lecturer, poetry teacher and journalist. She is best known for her genuine love of nature, so apparent in her work.

Miroslav Holub (1923–98) was a Czech poet and immunologist. He wrote many scientific essays and his poems are heavily influenced by his scientific knowledge.

A. E. Housman (1859–1936) was a British poet and pre-eminent classicist, gaining the prestigious position of the Kennedy Professor of Latin at Cambridge University in 1911. His most famous work is perhaps *A Shropshire Lad*, which has not been out of print since its original publication in 1896.

Ted Hughes (1930-98) was born in West Yorkshire and was a poet and children's writer. He was famously married to American poet Sylvia Plath until her suicide in 1963. He became Poet Laureate in 1984 and received the Order of Merit from the Queen just before his death.

Elizabeth Jennings (1926-2001) worked in advertising, in the city library and in publishing before becoming a full-time writer. An important theme in her work is Catholicism.

John Keats (1795-1821) was born in London and died at the age of just 25 in Rome from tuberculosis, a disease that had plagued his family. His initial medical ambitions were overtaken by his literary interests and despite his short life he has become recognised as the principal poet of the English Romantic movement.

Rudyard Kipling (1865-1936) was a British author and poet. He was born in India but spent much of his childhood in Portsmouth, where he stayed with a couple who cared for the children of British Nationals living in India. He is perhaps best known for writing *The Jungle Book* (Macmillan, 1894).

Philip Larkin (1922-85) is considered one of the greatest English poets of the 20th century. As well as writing, he spent his working life as a librarian. His poetry often celebrates everyday features of English life.

D. H. Lawrence (1885-1930) was an author, poet, playwright, essayist and literary critic. During his lifetime much of his work was considered pornographic; today he is seen as an important modernist figure.

Catherine Phil MacCarthy (1954-) is a poet and teacher of creative writing. She has written one very successful novel and is currently working on her second. Born in Crecora in County Limerick, she now lives in Dublin.

Louis MacNeice (1907-63) was an Irish poet and playwright. His relaxed style meant that he was very successful during his lifetime.

John Gillespie Magee (1922–41) was born in Shanghai, China. In 1939 he moved to the United States and joined the Royal Canadian Air Force. He was killed in a mid-air collision three days after the United States entered World War II. His poem *High Flight* was displayed in the Library of Congress in Washington after his death and remains there today.

Derek Mahon (1941–) is a poet and translator. Born in Belfast, he currently lives in Kinsale in County Cork. In 2001 he was awarded the David Cohen Prize for Literature.

Don Marquis (1878–1937) was an American humorist, journalist, novelist, poet and playwright. He is best-known for creating the characters of Archy, a poetic cockroach, and Mehitabel, an alley cat.

John Masefield (1878–1967) was a poet and novelist. He is particularly remembered as the author of some successful children's novels, including *The Midnight Folk* (Heinemann, 1927). In 1930 he was appointed Poet Laureate, a role he took very seriously, producing a large quantity of work.

F. R. McCreary was an American poet. In 1943 he joined Harvard University as an English teacher, teaching the many American troops who would be fighting in World War II.

Sue Minish was educated in England and Germany and is now living in the west of Ireland; she has been writing poetry and reviewing books for many years.

John Montague (1929–) was born in Brooklyn, New York but was sent to County Tyrone in Ireland at a very young age, so is considered by most to be an Irish poet. His work, however, displays American rather than British instincts. He currently lives in Cork.

Andrew Motion (1952–) lives in London and was recently appointed Professor of Creative Writing at Royal Holloway University, London. He is a fellow of the Royal Society of Literature and in 1999 began a 10-year stint as Poet Laureate.

Grace Nichols (1950-) was born in Guyana and much of her work, which includes poetry and stories for children, reflects her interest in Amerindian myths, Guyanese folk tales and the South American civilisations of the Aztec and Inca.

Gareth Owen (1936-2002) was a poet, novelist and broadcaster. His time as a teacher provided a huge source of inspiration for his work. He is perhaps best known for his children's poetry and his time on BBC Radio as the presenter of *Poetry Please!*

Brian Patten (1946-) is a Liverpool-born poet who divides his time between Devon and London. For more information, visit his website at http://www.brianpatten.co.uk.

Daniel Pettiward was a painter, writer, cartoonist, broadcaster and illustrator. He was the brother of the famous cartoonist Roger Pettiward, who worked under the name Paul Crum.

Cole Porter (1891-1964) was an American songwriter and musician who enjoyed huge success on Broadway and also wrote for some Hollywood greats, such as Frank Sinatra.

James Reeves (1909-78) is best known for his poetry and children's literature but also worked as a literary critic and broadcaster. He taught until 1952, before becoming a full-time writer.

Michael Rosen (1946-) was appointed as the Children's Laureate in 2007. He has written for TV and radio and is also well known as a vocal critic of the government's education policies.

David Rubadiri (1930-) is a poet, playwright and academic, and is Ambassador for Malawi to the United Nations.

Siegfried Sassoon (1886-1967) was born into a very wealthy Anglo-Jewish family. He began writing poetry before the outbreak of World War I but is remembered as a war poet; his work was transformed by what he saw during the war. His poems show a real empathy with the soldiers of the time, giving them a voice.

Vernon Scannell (1922-2007) served with the army during World War II and then had a brief career in boxing before turning to writing. He wrote both poetry and novels, and was also a critic, writing regular reviews for *Ambit* magazine and for the *Sunday Telegraph*.

Percy Bysshe Shelley (1792-1822) is a famous English poet, known for his poetry and political writing. Shelley was lost at sea in 1822.

Boris Slutsky (1919-86) was born in Slovyansk in the Ukraine. He served in the Red Army during World War II and later worked in radio. His first book of poetry, *Memory*, was published in 1957. After his death it was discovered that more than half his work had not been published.

Jean Sprackland (1962-) was born in Burton-on-Trent and taught for a short while before beginning to write poetry at the age of 30. She also offers training and consultancy to organisations such as the Poetry Society and Poetry Archive.

Muriel Stuart (1885-1967) was born in Norbury. Her poetry was initially influenced by the events of World War I but she later explored sexual politics in her work. Her most well-known, *In the Orchard* (Heinemann, 1922) is unusual in that it is purely dialogue rather than verse.

Rabindranath Tagore (1861-1941) was a Bengali poet, philosopher, artist, novelist and composer. He was educated at home and then sent to school in England. In 1913 he became the first Nobel Laureate in Asia when he won the Nobel Prize for Literature.

Edward Thomas (1878-1917) worked as a literary critic and produced poetry, a novel and various pieces of non-fiction, initially under the name Edward Easaway. He enlisted in the Army in 1915 and was killed in action during the Battle of Arras shortly after arriving in France.

Anthony Thwaite (1930-) was born in Chester and brought up in Yorkshire, although he was briefly evacuated to the United States during World War II. A poet himself, he is also one of the literary executors of Philip Larkin's work and has edited volumes of Larkin's poems.

Yevgeny Vinokurov (1925-93) was a Russian writer and poet. He was born in Bryansk into a family of career soldiers; between 1943 and 1946 he served as a paratrooper on the Ukrainian front. He later studied geology.

Richard Wilbur (1921-) was born in New York City. He has won the Pulitzer Prize for Poetry twice (1957 and 1989) and in 1987 was the second person to be named the United States Poet Laureate.

William Wordsworth (1770-1850) was orphaned at a young age and suffered several other personal tragedies during his life, including the death of his two illegitimate children. In his younger years he had many radical political views; however, he developed into a conservative poet most associated with the movement of Romanticism.

W. B. Yeats (1865-1939) was an Irish poet and dramatist. He had a particular interest in Irish history and mythology. In 1923 he was awarded the Nobel Prize for Literature.

Han Yong-Un (1897-1944) was a Korean Buddhist poet and a political leader. Born in northern Gyeongsang (now known as South Korea) he was ordained as a Buddhist monk in 1905.

Benjamin Zephaniah (1958-) was born in England, although he spent some of his childhood in his family's home in Jamaica. He is a well-known performance poet and novelist, and has written several books for young people, including *Face* (Bloomsbury, 1999) and *Gangsta Rap* (Bloomsbury, 2004).

Acknowledgements

The volume editor and publishers acknowledge the following sources of copyright material and are grateful for the permissions granted. While every effort has been made, it has not always been possible to identify the sources of all the material used, or to trace all copyright holders. If any omissions are brought to our notice we will be happy to include the appropriate acknowledgements on reprinting.

p. 1 lines from 'A Martian Sends a Postcard Home' by Craig Raine, copyright © Craig Raine, 1979; p. 3 'On my Short-Sightedness' by Prem Chaya; p. 4 'The Blind Man at the Fair' by Joseph Campbell; p. 6 'First Sight' by Philip Larkin from *The Whitsun Weddings*, published by Faber and Faber Ltd; p. 8 'Kob Antelope' translated by Ulli Beier; pp. 12, 39 'Red Kites Rising' and 'Unburglars' by Philip Gross from *The Egg of Zero* (Bloodaxe Books, 2006); pp. 14, 147 'Acts of God' and 'Charms' by Catherine Phil MacCarthy; p. 15 'Mawu of the Waters' by Abena P.A. Busia; p. 16 'The Ferryboat and the Traveller' by Han Yong-Un; pp. 17, 137 'The Fridge' and Untitled ('In a Non Sleeper') by Boris Slutsky, translated by Elaine Feinstein. Copyright © Anne Enright, reproduced by permission of the author c/o Rogers, Coleridge & White Ltd., 20 Powis Mews, London W11 1JN; pp. 18, 48, 55, 71, 89 'The Inside of Things', 'Bringing Up a Single Parent', 'Geography Lesson', 'My Neighbour's Rabbit' and 'Trees in the Storm' by Brian Patten Copyright © Brian Patten, reproduced by permission of the author c/o Rogers, Coleridge & White Ltd., 20 Powis Mews, London W11 1JN; p. 19 'The Seed Shop' by Muriel Stuart; pp. 20, 53 'Gunpowder Plot' and 'The Apple-raid' by Vernon Scannell; p. 22 'They' by Siegfried Sassoon Copyright Siegfried Sassoon, by kind permission of the Estate of George Sassoon; p. 33 'One' by James Berry from *When I Dance* (© James Berry 1988) is reproduced by permission of PFD (www.pfd.co.uk) on behalf of James Berry; p. 34 'Friendship' (from "DuBarry Was A Lady") words and music by Cole Porter © 1939 (renewed) Chappell & Co., Inc., all rights reserved, used by permission of Alfred Publishing Co. Inc.; p. 36 'Friendship' by Elizabeth Jennings published by Carcanet in *Collected Poems*; p. 37 'Heroes' by Benjamin Zephaniah, *Too Black, Too Strong* (Bloodaxe Books, 2003); p. 40 'Boy at the Window' from *Things of This World*, copyright © 1952 and renewed 1980 by Richard Wilbur, reprinted by permission of Houghton Mifflin

Harcourt Publishing company. This material may not be reproduced in any form or by any means without the prior written permission of the publisher. Published by Faber and Faber Ltd; p. 41 'Footings' from *The Heel of Bernadette* by Colette Bryce. Copyright © Colette Bryce, 2000; p. 42 'Purge' by Sheila Glen Bishop from *Snailshells or Butterflies*, published by the National Poetry Foundation, 1992; pp. 44, 45, 46, 82 'Sewing Fingertips', 'Shocks', 'Tell Your Mother I Saved Your Life' and 'Caravan' from *Hard Water* by Jean Sprackland, published by Jonathan Cape. Reprinted by permission of The Random House Group Ltd; p. 47 'Smothering Sunday' by John Hegley, from *The Family Pack*, published by Methuen Publishing Ltd; p. 49 'In the Playground' by Michael Rosen from *When Did You Last Wash Your Feet?* (© Michael Rosen 1986) is printed by permission of United Agents (www.uniteda gents.co.uk) on behalf of Michael Rosen; p. 50 'Conkers' by Grace Nichols Copyright © Grace Nichols 1989 reproduced with permission of Curtis Brown Group Ltd; p. 52 'The Shout' by Simon Armitage from *The Universal Home Doctor*, published by Faber & Faber Ltd; p. 56 'Mid-Term Break' by Seamus Heaney from *Death of a Naturalist*, published by Faber and Faber Ltd; pp. 57, 140 'Night Mail' and 'O What is That Sound' by W.H. Auden from *Collected Poems* ed. E. Mendelson, published by Faber and Faber Ltd Copyright © 1936 and © 1934 by W.H. Auden. Reprinted by permission of Curtis Brown, Ltd; p. 69 'The Door' by Miroslav Holub; p. 70 'Our Pond' by Daniel Pettiward; p. 72 'My Mother saw a Dancing Bear' by Charles Causley, published by Faber and Faber in *The Ring of Words*; p. 73 'Hedgehog' by Anthony Thwaite © the author, from Collected Poems (Enitharmon Press, 2007); p. 77 'The Fox' from *The Leave Train: New and Selected Poems* by Phoebe Hesketh (Enitharmon Press, 1994); p. 78 'An Old Woman of the Roads' by Pádraic Colum, used by permission of the Estate of Pádraic Colum; p. 81 'The Song of Wandering Aengus' by W.B. Yeats, from *Irish Poems for Young People* published by Wolfhound Press. Used by permission of A P Watt Ltd on behalf of Gráinne Yeats; p. 84 'The Bicycle' by Derek Mahon used by kind permission of the author and The Gallery Press, Loughcrew, Oldcastle, County Meath, Ireland from *Collected Poems* (1999); p. 86 'Wind Gauge' by Gillian Clarke, from *Collected Poems*, published by Carcanet Press Limited; p. 87 'Slowly, the Fog' by F.R. McCreary; p. 88 'Mist' by Douglas Gibson; p. 90 'Feeding out-wintering cattle at twilight' by Ted Hughes from *Moortown*, published by Faber and Faber Ltd; p. 101 'The Sea' © James Reeves from

Complete Poems for Children (Faber Finds), reprinted by permission of the James Reeves Estate. Anthology available at www.faber.co. uk/faberfinds; p. 102 'Sea Fever' by John Masefield, used by permission of The Society of Authors as the literary representative for the Estate of John Masefield; p. 103 'Thoughts Like an Ocean' Copyright © Gareth Owen, reproduced by permission of the author c/o Rogers, Coleridge & White Ltd., 20 Powis Mews, London W11 1JN; p. 105 'Evidence' by Eiléan Ní Chuilleanáin by permission of the author and The Gallery Press, Loughcrew, Oldcastle, County Meath, Ireland from *Acts and Monuments* (1972); p. 106 'Tree Stump' by Moya Cannon, by kind permission of the author and The Gallery Press, Loughcrew, Oldcastle, County Meath, Ireland, from *Oar* (2000); p. 107 'The Cherry Trees' by Laurence Binyon used by permission of The Society of Authors as the literary representative for the Estate of Laurence Binyon; p. 109 'Stopping by Woods on a Snowy Evening' from *The Poetry of Robert Frost*, edited by Edward Connery Lathem, published by Johnathan Cape. Reprinted by permission of The Random House Group Ltd' pp. 112, 132 'Uffington' and 'Five O'Clock Shadow' by John Betjeman; pp. 113, 131, 133 'Dumbshow', 'There Are Days' and 'Guardians' by John Montague used by kind permission of the author and The Gallery Press, Loughcrew, Oldcastle, County Meath, Ireland from *Smashing the Piano* (1999); p. 117 'In the Attic' by Andrew Motion from *Selected Poems 1976–1997*, published by Faber and Faber Ltd; p. 119 'High Flight' by John Gillespie Magee reproduced by kind permission of This England magazine; p. 120 '2000 A.D.' by Rabindranath Tagore, The Tagore Centre UK; p. 134 'A Dream' by Dermot Healy used by kind permission of the author and The Gallery Press, Loughcrew, Oldcastle, County Meath, Ireland from *What the Hammer* (1998); p. 136 'House on a Cliff' by Louis MacNeice, from *Collected Poems*, published by Faber and Faber Ltd; p. 138 'Missing the Troop Train' by Yevgeny Vinokurov, translated by Daniel Weissbort, Copyright © Daniel Weissbort, 1974, reproduced with permission of Johnson & Alcock Ltd; p. 142 'Stanley meets Mutesa' by David Rubadiri; p. 146 'Call to a Simple Feast' by S.M. Minish; p. 149 'Watching for Dolphins' by David Constantine, *Collected Poems* (Bloodaxe Books, 2004);

The publishers would like to thank the following for permission to reproduce photographs:

p. 10 Joe McDonald/Corbis; p. 35 FPG/Getty Images; p. 54 The Print Collector/Photolibrary; p. 83 Chris Howes/Wild Places Photography/ Alamy; p. 90 Paul C. Pet/Corbis; p. 116 Michael Kai/Corbis; p. 144 Boris Lyubner/Illustration Works/Corbis